# 31 DAYS to Becoming a BETTER RELIGIOUS EDUCATOR

"Jared Dees is one of the most gifted young catechetical leaders of our time. *31 Days to Becoming a Better Religious Educator*—full of inspiration and practical insight—is a wonderful gift to the Church."

**Rev. Timothy R. Scully, C.S.C.**
Founder of Alliance for Catholic Education
University of Notre Dame

"Dees offers practical ideas and simple exercises for deepening your faith and improving your performance as a teacher/catechist. It's boot camp basics for a new teacher and offers new and improved techniques for veteran catechists. You won't be disappointed. Two pages a day for a month and if you only make one change, I guarantee you will be happier and so will your students. Read it, start exercising the idea, and it will become part of your DNA of teaching. It's simple but essential on the road to being a great catechist who connects head, heart, and hands—both yours and theirs. Dees has taken our basic desire to improve, combined it with the essentials of good teaching, mingled in the core elements of a good spiritual life, and added a dose of servant leadership to create a self-help book for both initial teachers and long-time catechists. It's an easy read with practical exercises to maximize your potential for success."

**Leland Nagel**
Executive Director
National Conference for Catechetical Leadership

"The chapters of this book have very practical concepts and ideas for catechists, but more importantly, the 'going deeper' section brings in an applicable spiritual dimension."

**Sr. Margaret Kuntz, A.S.C.J.**
Director of the Office of Catechesis
Diocese of Pensacola-Tallahassee

"The strength of any Catholic school lies in the ability of its teachers to deliver and communicate our faith with enthusiasm and personal witness. *31 Days to Becoming a Better Religious Educator* offers encouragement and practical advice to religious educators in order to better serve their students and enhance their own abilities as Catholic school teachers."

**Diane Starkovich**
Superintendent of Schools
Archdiocese of Atlanta

"A handy and practical tool from an emerging voice in religious education for enriching and enlivening faith development."

**Gerard F. Baumbach**
Senior Catechetical Advisor
Institute for Church Life
University of Notre Dame

"Jared Dees has created an exciting and superbly practical field guide for those who love the Catholic faith and have a passion for effective teaching."

**Lisa Mladinich**
Author of *Be an Amazing Catechist*

"You can always spot someone who is a natural teacher, and Jared Dees fits the description. Dees understands the ins and outs of the religious education classroom and offers tried-and-true strategies for helping religious educators more effectively share information with and spiritually form their students."

**Joe Paprocki**
Author of *The Catechist's Toolbox*

"Jared Dees is one of the most innovative catechists writing today. He brings his considerable knowledge and experience to bear in *31 Days to Becoming a Better Religious Educator*. Even the most veteran catechists are sure to find valuable insights, tips, and advice to help them in their ministry."

**Jonathan Sullivan**
Director of Catechetical Services
Diocese of Springfield in Illinois

"Dees offers an extensive collection of simple, practical, and well-researched ideas and strategies for becoming effective catechists in parish faith formation programs and religion teachers in Catholic schools.

"*31 Days to Becoming a Better Religious Educator* can be used individually, in small groups, and for in-service programs. It is for beginning and veteran catechists/religion teachers and helps them develop clear and practical plans for nurturing the spiritual formation of their students at the elementary, junior high, and senior high levels."

**Daniel J. Pierson**
Coauthor of *What Do I Do Know?: A Guide for the Reluctant Catechist*

"As a religious educator, one who supports catechists in my work, and especially as a mom—and thus as the primary faith formation teacher for my sons—I am thrilled to have Jared Dees's tremendous new resource, *31 Days to Becoming a Better Religious Educator*, in my arsenal. Dees shows each of us a manageable path toward becoming more effective in our sharing of the faith with those we serve. This book belongs in every Catholic parish, classroom, and home."

**Lisa M. Hendey**
Author of *A Book of Saints for Catholic Moms*

"This is a thoroughly practical, modern methodology grounded in Scripture and oriented toward the spiritual. Jared Dees defines what Catholic religious education needs to be."

**Marc Cardaronella**
Director of Religious Education
Holy Cross Church, Champaign, IL

"Jared Dees provides a terrific resource for catechists and teachers not only on how to bear great fruit in the classroom, but also on how they are called to be spiritually nourished in their ministry of passing on the faith in the third millennium. This will be a valuable resource not just to read once, but to constantly come back to and be encouraged, challenged, and inspired."

**William O'Leary**
Director of Religious Formation
Church of the Ascension

# 31 DAYS to Becoming a BETTER RELIGIOUS EDUCATOR

**Jared Dees**

ave maria press AmP notre dame, indiana

Founded in 1865, Ave Maria Press is a ministry of the United States Province of Holy Cross.

www.avemariapress.com

Paperback: ISBN-10 1-59471-384-7, ISBN-13 978-1-59471-384-2

E-book: ISBN-10 1-59471-385-5, ISBN-13 978-1-59471-385-9

Cover image © Getty Images.

Cover and text design by Andy Wagoner.

Printed and bound in the United States of America.

*Library of Congress Cataloging-in-Publication Data is available.*

# Contents

# Foreword

In my travels around the country, speaking to catechists and catechetical leaders, I like to ask my audiences to indicate how many years they have been serving as catechists: first year? five years? ten? fifteen? twenty? Typically, I'll find someone who has twenty plus years of teaching experience. Once, however, as I went through this routine, one woman's hand remained in the air: thirty, thirty-five, forty, forty-five, fifty, fifty-five . . . I finally gave up and just asked her how many years she had been serving as a catechist. She proudly announced, "sixty years!" She had been a catechist longer than I had been alive. What was even more impressive, however, was the fact that, here she was, attending a workshop to learn practical skills for teaching the Catholic faith! She gets it: The most effective religion teachers are those who never tire of looking for, acquiring, and implementing practical skills and strategies for teaching the faith.

Jared Dees gets that as well. He knows that practical ideas help bring the faith to life and that parish catechists and Catholic school religion teachers are in need of practical strategies for catechizing effectively. I have no doubt that, like that woman I met at one of my workshops, Jared will still be excitedly pursuing the latest practical teaching strategies when he's in his sixth decade of teaching!

It is Jared's practicality, combined with his deep faith, that I find so compelling and inspiring. I have closely watched Jared's career in catechetical ministry, happily observing him evolve into one of the bright young "stars" on the catechetical scene. I have had the pleasure of knowing Jared for a number of years now and always enjoy meeting him out on the speaker's circuit where I am glad to say, he is making a name for himself as one of the most sought-after speakers in the field of catechesis.

Now, Jared brings all of this—his practicality, depth, youthful enthusiasm, and creativity—to this book, *31 Days to Becoming a Better Religious Educator*, which he aptly describes as providing "practical tips for improving your teaching skills and growing deeper in your relationship with Christ." Jared balances the need for effective teaching strategies and skills with the call to serve as a disciple of Jesus Christ. He has a clear sense of the vocation of the catechist and adds to that the professionalism that he himself has learned as an educator.

Even Jared's organization of this book is practical. He identifies and organizes the roles of the religious educator accordingly: the religious educator as . . .

- Disciple
- Servant
- Leader
- Teacher

He skillfully takes each of these roles and further breaks them down into daily exercises to help religious educators reflect on their vocation and develop their skills.

Perhaps the most important thing about Jared, and about this book, is the fact that he recognizes where the "spotlight" is supposed to shine: not on ourselves as religious educators, but on those we teach and especially on the One whom we are proclaiming. Jared is not flashy and does not draw attention to himself. He is not a showboat. Likewise, his teaching strategies are not designed to turn the religious educator into an entertainer. Rather, he shows how to polish your technique so that, like a window that is polished, others are able to see through you to what lies beyond, namely, the presence of Jesus Christ in our midst. By encouraging us to be more effective religious educators, Jared, paradoxically, shows us how to "get out of the way" of the Holy Spirit, who is the true Teacher.

As someone who has been "in the business" for over thirty years, written many books, done numerous presentations, and hosted my own blog on catechesis, I know good catechesis when I see it. Jared Dees is the real deal. I have no doubt that you will find inspiration and support in his *31 Days to Becoming a Better Religious Educator.*

Oh, and one more thing. I have no doubt that, when Jared reaches his sixtieth year as a catechist, he'll still be flashing that same boyish grin that lights up a room and let's people know that they are about to encounter the Good News!

Joe Paprocki, DMin

# Introduction

*"Go, therefore, and make disciples of all nations, bap-
tizing them in the name of the Father, and of the Son,
and of the holy Spirit, teaching them to observe all
that I have commanded you. And behold, I am with
you always, until the end of the age." (Mt 28:19–20)*

Jesus spoke these words to the Apostles, but he also speaks
to us. We have been called and sent to the classroom to
make disciples. As Christ's disciples, we are called to make
disciples of others. In the name of the Father, Son, and
Holy Spirit, we go and we teach. Each one of us has been
given the gifts to change the lives of the young people
we serve. Do we realize the full scope of that responsibility? Are we taking steps to become the best religious educators we can be?

This book is designed with thirty-one days of exercises
and spiritual practices to help you become a better religious
educator. Whether you are new to catechesis or a seasoned
veteran, each of these exercises will help you hone your
skills and let your gifts shine before the students you teach.

Whether you are in a Catholic school or a parish religious education program, you will be able to find practical tips for improving your teaching skills and growing deeper in your relationship with Christ.

## The Church Needs You

Our call to teach faith comes at a critical moment in the Church's history. The Church is losing her members. People are trading their selfless spirituality for self-help and a personalized faith. They are seeking God (though they do not know it) in all the wrong places.

The *National Directory for Catechesis* points out a number of challenges to catechesis, including secularism, religious indifference, unengaged adults, unaffiliated young adults, and the significant number of young people who are not enrolled in Catholic schools or parish religious education programs (*National Directory for Catechesis*, 13). There is no assurance that the students who enter our Catholic schools and parish religious education programs today will call themselves Catholics when they grow up. The number of ex-Catholics in the United States, if they formed a religious group, would be the second or third largest denomination in the country.

Do not lose hope. As Pope John Paul II wrote, "I plead with you—never, ever give up on hope, never doubt, never tire, and never become discouraged. Be not afraid." These challenges of our culture and society should not cause us to lose hope, nor should we expect to change the course of history all on our own. What we can do now is be the best inspiration possible for the students and the faith community we serve by becoming better at what we do each day by the grace of God.

The challenges of our culture are not insurmountable. We can fight them by becoming better at our work of evangelization and catechesis. With Christ as our inspiration, the practical tips and exercises in this book will help you to do your part as a catechist to make a more powerful impact on the lives of your students. The thirty-one days of exercises in this book are organized around four distinct yet well-connected roles of a religious educator.

## Four Roles of Religious Educators

To be a religious educator, we must embrace several unique roles. These are different roles from those who teach other subjects like math or science. To be a Christian religious educator, or specifically a Catholic religious educator, we must embrace our common vocation and identity to live and share the Gospel given to us at Baptism. The thirty-one days of exercises in this book are organized around four roles of a Catholic religious educator, one building on the next:

First, you must be a *great disciple*. You must follow and learn from Christ.

You must also be a *great servant*. You must selfishly set aside your own desires to serve others.

Only as disciples and servants can you become a *great leader*. Jesus said, "The Son of Man did not come to be served, but to serve and to give his life as a ransom for many" (Mk 10:45).

These three roles—disciple, servant, and leader—all help to make a *great teacher*. Jesus is the Master Teacher: "You call me 'teacher' and 'master' and rightly so, for indeed I am" (Jn 13:13). We are called to imitate Jesus and make these roles our own. Let's explore each role a bit more.

## Becoming a Better Disciple

Jesus commands us to "go and make disciples of all nations . . ." We are called to be disciples and to make disciples of the students we teach. Someone at one time or another inspired us to follow Christ, and someone inspired them to follow Christ too. Through our work as religion teachers and catechists, we inspire our students to follow Christ, but in so doing we do not cease to be disciples ourselves.

There is truth in a common saying: The best teachers are students. Teachers who themselves have a passion for learning also have a passion for teaching. Get teachers talking about their subject over a cup of coffee, and they will talk your ear off. They are filled with a hunger and thirst to read and learn as much as they can about their subject, not only to be able to better present their lessons, but for the sake of learning itself.

In religious education this means more than just learning the content of the faith. Good religion teachers and catechists develop a hunger not only to learn about God, but also to come to know God more. The path of discipleship is inspired by the loving call of God and matured through constant learning and self-development. In other words, for a teacher to be a disciple, he or she must learn the content of the faith, but more importantly spend time in prayer, experience the sacraments, strive to live a moral life, and participate in a community of faith.

What can a teacher do to become a better disciple? To put it simply, follow Christ. "Listen to him," as the Father said at his Transfiguration (Lk 9:35), and, as Mary said to the servants at the wedding feast in Cana, "Do whatever he tells you" (Jn 2:5). Like Jesus, we must humble ourselves. Quoting John 7:16, Pope John Paul II wrote, "Every catechist should be able to apply to himself the mysterious words of Jesus: 'My teaching is not mine, but his who sent me.'" (*Catechesi Tradendae*, 6).

In part I, we will look to many sources to teach us: our life experiences, our favorite teachers, the Scriptures, the saints, our students, and of course, Christ himself. Each of these days will have a common goal: to help us humble ourselves as teachers and always seek to be better learners, better disciples.

## Becoming a Better Servant

In writing about the Sonship of Jesus, Pope Benedict XVI once pointed out, "As king he is servant, and as servant of God he is king" (*Introduction to Christianity*, 220). St. Paul quotes one of the earliest hymns about Jesus in his Letter to the Philippians: "He emptied himself, taking the form of a slave" (Phil 2:7). Following Christ's example, we, too, must become servants in order to be leaders.

We must follow Jesus' command to love as he loved. Taking on the disposition of a servant changes the way we look at our duties. We react differently to challenges and failures when we recognize that as educators we meet our students' greatest needs. Our task as servants is to recognize their needs and selflessly seek to address them in unique ways.

In part II, you will focus on putting yourself into a self-giving frame of mind. These days are about shifting your focus away from yourself and onto your students.

You will look closely at your students' needs and strengths. You will spend time getting to know your students on a more personal level. You will praise and pray for students and further develop your relationship with your students' parents.

## Becoming a Better Leader

The greatest leaders in history have a way of commanding our attention by earning trust and respect from those that follow them. Leadership also requires action. A selfless disposition of service is the key to earning this trust. Carving a path through difficult situations is also required for good leadership. It requires the organized and simple presentation of a path toward a common goal. The clarity with which great leaders can communicate their vision is a key component to their skill.

Jesus showed us the way. He never said it would be easy. He led by the ultimate example, laying down his life for us. And, he told us to take up our crosses as well. He formed his disciples as leaders and sent them out with the help of the Holy Spirit. They, in turn, carried forth his message and changed the lives of the people they encountered.

Part III is devoted to helping you to become a better leader. You will examine practical skills of leadership: classroom organization, discipline, and motivation. How well you master these tasks contributes to your students growing closer to God and learning more about their faith.

## Becoming a Better Teacher

Jesus is called "teacher" forty-two times and "rabbi" fourteen times in the New Testament. Clearly, teaching is a significant part of his identity, as it is a part of ours as religious educators. Jesus taught more than just the content of the faith, more than just abstract truths about theology. Through his teaching he shared the mystery of himself.

How did he do it? As the *National Directory for Catechesis* explains, "Christ's methodology was multi-dimensional. It included his words, his signs, and the wonders he worked" (92). In a similar way, as religious educators we appeal to a variety of methods to teach our students. We use words, images, music, movement, and our own lives as examples to teach. Pope John Paul II called for a catechesis that is "systematic, not improvised but programmed to reach a precise goal" (*Catechesi Tradendae*, 21).

The exercises in part IV are devoted to helping you think systematically about how you approach your work. You will find tips on setting and assessing mastery of learning objectives and examples of how to reach those objectives using story, textbooks, projects, music, and movement. You will spend some time reflecting on and improving your lesson plans and class activities. Most importantly, you will become what you are meant to be: a witness to the Gospel. This is the true vocation of every religious educator.

## Making the Journey through *31 Days to Becoming a Better Religious Educator*

Recall Christ's words to his Apostles during the Great Commission: "I am with you always until the end of the age." Throughout this book you will participate in exercises to realize this presence within you and share it with others. This process of becoming disciple-teachers and servant-leaders is the spiritual journey of the religious educator.

Are you ready to take on this thirty-one-day journey to becoming the best religious educator you can be? The material fits naturally into one month. You may wish to do all thirty-one days on consecutively, doubling up some days to take a break on the weekends. Or you can allot one day per week to do an exercise and finish the week roughly over the course of two semesters. Although many of the days are closely connected with the others and build on one another, you could certainly pick and choose certain exercises to do at any time throughout the year. Keep in mind that the exercises in the first three parts of this book are focused on forming you as a person, so they work best if done in preparation for the exercises in Part IV. There is nothing more important that you can do for your students than focusing on yourself as a committed disciple, servant, and leader.

Teachers and catechists are some of the busiest people I know, so the daily exercises are designed to take around ten to fifteen minutes to complete. Some of the days may strike a cord more than others and inspire you to spend more time on them. If there is a certain exercise that really gets you thinking creatively and working productively, then give it the necessary time to make an impact on your work in religious education. Each of the thirty-one days is organized as follows:

- There is a **Scripture passage** to connect the theme of the exercise and to encourage prayerful reflection as you begin.

- A short **introduction** to the day's exercise follows. It explains why the topic is important to religious educators. The format of the introduction includes stories from my own experience as both a Catholic school religion teacher and a parish catechist. Other examples are based in the Scriptures, the lives of the saints, and in the research of educational psychologists. Because some of the examples and stories in this book are directed toward religious educators in two different settings, some of the language and directives may not apply to you as much as to others.

- Next a practical, **daily exercise** is intended to help you improve on one or more skills for becoming a better religious educator. There are step-by-step descriptions of the tasks required to carry out the exercise, so implementing them each day should be very manageable. Many of the exercises require reflection, so consider using a journal to follow along with this book.

- Finally, at the end of each exercise there is an additional opportunity for "**going deeper**" in prayer, reflection, or meditation on Scripture. As religious educators, we need to spend time listening and learning from God in prayer and reflection in order to be the best disciple-teachers and servant-leaders we can be.

The best way to ensure you start and finish this thirty-one-day journey is to pick a consistent time of day to go through each daily exercise. The consistency will help you remember to pick up this book and go through each exercise.

## Online Support

My intention is for *31 Days to Becoming a Better Religious Educator* to be a living document, with the ability to expand the support you are able to receive as a religious educator. Please visit my website at www.thereligionteacher.com/31days for extra tips, resources, and downloads. You can also sign up for an online reminder to stay on your own schedule as you navigate the thirty-one days.

May God bless you and bless your ministry.

Go and make disciples!

# Part I

# **Become a Better Disciple**

# Day 1

# **Recall Your Calling as a Religious Educator**

*"As each one has received a gift, use it to serve one another as good stewards of God's varied grace." (1 Pt 4:10)*

Whether you have chosen this ministry as a career or you are volunteering your time to the Church, your work as a religious educator is a calling from God. Blessed Basil Moreau, founder of the Congregation of Holy Cross, pointed out that "since God alone provides the means for the successful accomplishment of any task, it seems evident that a person needs to be called by God to be an effective teacher" (*Christian Education*). The *National Directory for Catechesis* echoes Moreau's words: "The call to the ministry of catechist is a vocation, an interior call, the voice of the Holy Spirit" (228).

On the first day of this thirty-one-day journey, you will take some time to listen to the voice of the Holy Spirit and consider how you have been called to teach the faith. Understanding the *why* behind your work as a religious educator is absolutely essential because while the challenges of evangelization and catechesis are many and immediate, their rewards are mostly long-term. The joy in doing the work must push you through the good times and the bad. Basil Moreau put it more bluntly: "Without this call to teaching, how will anyone be able to put up with everything that teachers face daily?"

Teaching—especially teaching religion—is challenging. It can come with all sorts of doubts, both from students and from within ourselves. However, do not be discouraged. Recognize that catechesis is a calling from God and that together as a Church we go forth in passionate pursuit of God's will.

How do we recognize God's call? Usually, we do not hear God's voice in a dream like the prophet Samuel (1 Sm 3:1–18), and we are unlikely to find any burning bushes like Moses (Ex 3) any time soon. Rather than waiting for a magnificently profound sign, we can find our calling in both what we love to do and in the needs of those who require our love the most.

In many of the examples of God's calling in the Bible, the focus is more upon the needs of the people who will be ministered to rather than the skills, talents, and experience of those who were being called. For example, Moses was not eloquent in speech, yet he was called to speak to the Pharaoh about securing the release of the Israelites from Egypt. Peter was just a fisherman Jesus called by the Sea of Galilee, but he became the leader of the Church. David was just a young boy with a slingshot, yet he was called to defeat a great warrior, Goliath.

In each of these stories, there is a great need, and God calls individuals to meet these needs despite their lack of personal talents, skills, abilities, and experience. When they succeed, they do so because of their faith in God's assistance. Whether you are a first-year teacher or catechist or someone with years of teaching experience, God sends you a call to meet his children's greatest needs and supports you in the work.

Our mission as religious educators is important to the Church's mission of evangelization. So many Catholics are leaving the Church because they misunderstand the Church's teachings. Many of our students' parents do not take their children to Mass on Sundays. Morality is derived more from psychology than theology. Prayer is seen as something only grandmothers do. It is to these desperate needs that you are being called to religious education. You will not be able to solve all of the Church's challenges on your own, but know that these needs are out there. The question for today's exercise is which need are you being called to address the most? What do you see as the biggest challenge for your students?

## Exercise: Define Your Calling to the Classroom

Make a list of the needs that you are most passionate about addressing through your work as a religious educator. This is your "Big Why List." When teaching gets tough and you just don't seem to be getting through to your students, review and remember this list. Your Big Why List is a great indicator of your calling.

Use the following questions to develop your Big Why List:

- If I had to choose just one lesson about God that my students need to hear the most, what would it be?

- What is one belief my students struggle with the most?

- What is one spiritual practice my students could benefit from the most?

- If I could help my students make one change in their lives, what would it be?

- What aspect of the faith are kids missing the most in their lives?

- What are the biggest problems adult Catholics experience in the Church?

Star or circle the answers that either get you excited or make you angry. If there is only one answer that gets you really excited, then consider this the focal point of your call to teach. These great needs are placed upon your heart as a calling from God. You are in a special position to meet these needs in your role as religious educator.

When I completed this exercise, my list had problems like "kids don't know how to pray on their own" and "kids misunderstand the meanings of sin and grace." The thing that gets me really fired up, though, is a simple statistic: "one out of every ten Americans is an ex-Catholic" (*Pew Forum on Religion and Public Life*). Since many of these ex-Catholics were once enrolled in religious education programs and attended Catholic schools as children, I see this as a problem I can address in the classroom. Like many other religion teachers and catechists, I want to share my passion for the Catholic faith so that others can develop a similar love for God and the Church. This desire is what gets me through the difficult times as a teacher and catechist. This need is so great that I cannot help but push through the daily roadblocks and challenges of religious education.

What about you? What gets you fired up? What part of the world needs changing the most, and how can you incorporate that into your call to the classroom? Go through the questions listed here and spend some time considering the ones that clearly reveal what God has placed on your heart as a need you must address.

## Going Deeper

Read one of the stories of God calling out leaders in the Bible, such as Samuel (1 Sm 3:1–18), Moses (Ex 3), Jonah (Jon 1), the Apostles (Mt 4:18–22), Matthew (Mt 9:9–13), and Paul (Acts 9:1–22). Ask yourself:

- What did these people feel passionate about?
- What aspect of their calling kept them going when things did not go well and when times were rough?

# Day 2

# Recognize Your Relationship with Christ

*"Who do you say that I am?" (Mk 8:29)*

As the *National Directory for Catechesis* suggests, catechists' "personal relationship with Jesus Christ energizes their service to the Church and provides continuing motivation, vitality, and force of their catechetical activity" (229). Not only are we called to the classroom with a *purpose* (Day 1), we are called there by a *person*. Without Christ at the center of our ministry as religious educators, we will not be able to participate in the spiritual growth of our students.

Catechesis is about more than knowing information; it is about knowing a person. Pope John Paul II expressed it best when he wrote, "the definitive aim of catechesis is to put people not only in touch with but in communion, in intimacy, with Jesus Christ (*Catechesi Tradendae*, 5). Recognizing where you are in your own relationship with Christ and taking steps toward deepening that relationship will help you through that process. The most important thing you do as a Catholic religious educator is to introduce your students to Christ and help them to foster a relationship with him.

In order to put others in communion and intimacy with Jesus Christ, you must first seek this intimacy with him yourself. It is not enough to just be in touch with your beliefs about Christ; you have to be in touch with the person of Christ. You need to come to know Christ in new ways and go deeper in your relationship with him by opening up in trust and curiosity to his will for you.

## Exercise: Recognize Your Relationship with Christ

Whenever we meet another married couple for the first time or participate in a marriage encounter at our parish, my wife and I usually get to tell the story about how we first met and how our relationship blossomed into marriage. Sharing the memories of how we met, dated, got engaged, and were married always gets us engergized about our relationship. Sharing these special memories reminds us why we first chose to love each other and commit ourselves to each other.

In this exercise, you are g
story about how you met Jes
grow in intimacy with him.
journal, describe your relat
following writing prompts

12

- **First, write how you met Jesus ᴏ**
  your first memory of him? How were you introduced to him? How long have you known him?
  What is one of your earliest memories of him?

- **Next, write about the ways you got to know
  Jesus more deeply.** Did you go to a Catholic
  school? Were you enrolled in a parish religious
  education program? Were you involved in youth
  ministry? Did you participate in a catechumenate
  process? Was your family influential in helping you
  get to know Christ? Did a husband, wife, or friend
  help you to get to know him more?

- **Finally, write about your current relationship
  with Jesus.** How often do you spend time with
  him in prayer? When do you pray? Where do
  you pray? How do you pray? Do you get to know
  him more by reading the Bible? Do you keep him
  in mind throughout your day? How does the

arist or the Sacrament of Reconciliation help
u grow closer to him?

Write in whatever format you find fits with your personality. You can write in paragraph form or make a random list. You can draw a timeline of your life and describe memories of certain occasions you were most aware of Jesus' presence. You can also use drawings to illustrate these memories if you are a visual learner.

Finally, review what you have written. Imagine that Christ is there with you having a conversation. Talk to him about these memories. Recount the memories with him as if you were recounting stories with an old friend. End with a prayer of thanksgiving for his presence in your life.

## Going Deeper

Choose a person in the New Testament who had a relationship with Jesus (Mary, Joseph, Peter, Paul, Lazarus, Zacchaeus, the woman at the well, etc.). Read a story about an interaction between them and consider how your relationship with Jesus is both similar and different. Ask yourself: Is there room for me to grow in deeper intimacy with the Lord as these first disciples and other saints have done?

# Day 3

# Imitate One of the Best Teachers in Your Life

*"Join with others in being imitators of me, brothers, and observe those who thus conduct themselves according to the model you have in us." (Phil 3:17)*

All of us have teachers who have made lasting impressions on our lives. Some of these men and women were the inspirations we needed to recognize our own call to become religious educators. Like Christ, they are models for how we can better touch the lives of the young people we serve.

St. Francis Xavier once wrote a letter to a fellow Jesuit priest to challenge him to humbly improve his work through the imitation of their common teacher and leader, St. Ignatius Loyola. "What you should have done was first to imitate the good works of our Father [Ignatius], and try to win those more excellent graces of his which moved our Lord God to give him such favor in the sight of all men" (*The Life and Letters of St. Francis Xavier*, 421).

As learners ourselves, we are called to humbly take in the lessons from the best teachers in our lives and apply them to our own work as religious educators. Using the best teaching styles and the most effective practices of our favorite teachers can help us to impact the lives of our own students.

## Exercise: Recalling a Favorite Teacher

Think back on your favorite teachers. These can be teachers in religious education classes, certainly, but also teachers and coaches from other subject areas too. What was it about them that allowed them to have such a lasting impact on you as a student? Next, focus on the strengths of a single teacher who made a big impact on your life. Plan to adapt this teacher's strengths to your own practice as a religious educator. Recall this teacher's presence in the classroom and some specific teaching techniques he or she used that made a big impact on you. Consider the following ways to recall why this teacher was so good at what he or she did:

- **Make a list of the teacher's most memorable lessons.** Be as specific as you can. For example, write something like, "I can still remember the drawing Mr. Heydinger made on the chalkboard to illustrate the symbolism within the first chapter of *The Lord of the Flies*."

- **Describe how the teacher kept the students' attention.** Was the teacher particularly funny? Did he connect personally with the students each day by name? My English teacher, Mr. Heydinger, was an excellent storyteller. His stories were not always on topic, but he was able to captivate the class's attention with unexpected jokes and memorable imagery.

- **Describe how the teacher assessed learning.** We are all familiar with tests. Tests come in all shapes and sizes, some with multiple-choice items and others with long essay questions. For me, the most memorable teachers made the assessment experience a part of the learning process. We were challenged on a daily basis to process, repeat, and apply what we had learned. What are some of the most memorable projects or assignments that you completed in your model teacher's class? What did your teacher add to these assignments that made them so interesting and engaging?

- **Describe how the teacher made you feel.** Some of the best teachers have a gift for making us feel confident about ourselves. These are the people who saw something in us and encouraged us to grow in some way, maybe even suggesting that we could one day become teachers. What did your teacher do to make you feel good about yourself and your work?

Once you have identified some of the qualities, techniques, and approaches to teaching that had a lasting impact on you as a student, choose at least one idea you could adapt to your own approach to education. Make a commitment to integrating this idea in the coming weeks. Make sure to write the idea you chose into a lesson plan or make a note of it on the cover page of a semester planner so that you won't forget.

## Going Deeper

As his Mother, Mary was the first teacher in Jesus' life. She modeled the way he should live his life. The best clue as to the type of teacher Mary would have been to her Son is her deeply humble disposition to God's will in the Magnificat (Lk 1:46–55). Pray the words of the Magnificat. Reflect on some ways you can apply what she said to your own life.

# Day 4

# **Spend Time Reading the Scriptures**

---

*"All Scripture is inspired by God and is useful for teaching, for refutation, for correction, and for training in righteousness, so that one who belongs to God may be competent, equipped for every good work."*
*(2 Tm 3:16–17)*

St. Augustine is known as one of the greatest Catholic theologians. He was a prolific writer and gifted orator. He was also an inspiring teacher. But earlier in his life Augustine was not a devout Christian. He rejected moral Christian living and led a life of sin. It was not until he had a profound experience with the Bible that he finally dedicated his life fully to the Church.

Through the intercession of his dedicated mother, St. Monica, and the life-changing inspiration of his teacher, St. Ambrose, St. Augustine was on the path of purity. He was praying in a garden one day when he heard a child's voice singing the lyrics "take and read." Grabbing his bible, he turned randomly to the Letter to the Romans and read a passage that changed his life. Afterward he recounted, "At once, with the last words of this sentence, it was as if a light of relief from all anxiety flooded into my heart. All the shadows of doubt were dispelled" (*Confessions*, Chapter 8).

Scripture has the power to transform us, whether we realize it or not. The Word of God is alive and inspired by the Holy Spirit. Unlike any other text, God is alive and active in Scripture. The Bible can transform us even if we feel like we do not get anything out of reading it or praying its words.

Modern approaches to reading the Bible tend to suggest that the more time we spend in the footnotes of our bibles, which can sometimes dominate the page, the more we will understand the *real* meaning behind the words. No, the power of the Word of God goes beyond the footnotes and literal meaning of the text. The actual verses have the power to meet us where we are and lead us to a deeper relationship with the Lord and on the path to his Kingdom. Spending time with God in prayerful reading of Scripture will help us to know him and his will more deeply.

# Exercise: Read the Scriptures

In today's exercise you will spend time reading the Bible. But here are some ground rules: You will be reading as a *disciple*, not a teacher. You will *not* be searching for lessons to teach your students. Rather, you will be opening up the Bible in order to have a personal encounter with God. You will be reading *and* praying. So turn off your lesson radar for a little bit and take on the perspective of a disciple.

Consider using the following approaches to encountering God in Scripture that are loosely based on the rich Catholic tradition of lectio divina:

- **Read it twice or more.** Focus on a short passage. Read it two or more times and see what jumps out at you and makes you think. Connect the passages with your own personal experiences of the day or recent weeks. This strategy is one way that helps God to meet us where we are in our lives. When we read a passage multiple times, our experiences tend to surface and connect with what we read.

- **Focus on one word or phrase.** What spiked your attention? Which words or phrases jump out at you during the first time you read it? During the second time? Focus on one word or phrase that really speaks to your heart. Choose a word or phrase that evokes a feeling or gets your mind thinking about your life. Usually this is God nudging you in a certain direction.

- **Put yourself in place of a person in the passage.** One of the most important skills in reading the Bible is to be able to deeply relate to the people in the stories. For example, imagine yourself as Peter during the Transfiguration. Or be one of the disciples and let Jesus wash your feet. How would seeing Jesus on the cross make you feel if you were a Roman centurion? Allow these experiences to transform your life.

- **Talk to Jesus about what you have read.** Be candid and honest with him about how you feel when reading this passage. Speak to Jesus as though you were having a conversation with him. Imagine Jesus sitting next to you. Tell him what you think and feel.

- **Just listen.** Sometimes the best way to encounter the Lord in Scripture is to just listen. Read the passage and just wait. Wait to see what pops into your head. Wait to hear the inner voice that tells you something you need to hear. This takes discipline and time. It requires us to empty our minds of what we *want* to hear and open ourselves up to what we *need* to hear.

How should you choose a Scripture passage? The lectionary of the Church has daily readings that progress through the entire Bible in a three-year period. This is a great tool to use. You can find these readings on the United States Conference of Catholic Bishops website (www.usccb.org).

You can also select a passage randomly based on whatever catches your eye as you thumb through the pages of the Bible. The Gospels are at the core of our faith, so they are a great place to focus your attention. The letters of the New Testament are instructive and inspirational as well. You might also read and pray with the Psalms, which have been the inspiration for personal and public prayer in the Church since her earliest days.

You can also draw on the suggested Scripture passages in the "Going Deeper" sections at the end of each chapter. Use these passages as a springboard to praying with the Bible. You can also come back to them later and see how God would like to touch your life through his Holy Word.

## Going Deeper

Choose one of the Psalms. Read it several times. Read it out loud. Pray with it. Do not try to interpret the meaning. Just listen to how the words speak to you. Imagine yourself singing these words as Jews and Christians throughout the ages have done. For example, pray with Psalm 23 and call on God as your own Good Shepherd.

# Day 5

# Spend Time Reading
# the Writings of a Saint

*"Attend to the reading, exhortation, and teaching. . . .
Attend to yourself and to your teaching; persevere in
both tasks, for by doing so you will save both yourself
and those who listen to you." (1 Tm 4:13, 16)*

On Day 3 we looked to the great teachers in our lives. On Day 4 we examined the importance of reading from Scripture. Today we will combine both exercises and spend time getting to know one of the great teachers of the Church, St. Benedict of Nursia, and take up his command to make the reading of spiritual teachers an even more central part of our lives.

St. Benedict lived in the fifth century. He was the son of a Roman noble who gave up his father's wealth with a mind to serve only God. He founded the Benedictine order and twelve communities for monks, including the famous

Monte Cassino in the mountains of southern Italy. He is also known as the "father of western monasticism."

In *The Rule of Saint Benedict*, the foundational text of almost every Catholic monastic tradition, St. Benedict requires that reading be an integral part of each and every day. He writes, "Idleness is the enemy of the soul; and therefore the brethren ought to be employed in manual labor at certain times, at others, in devout reading" (*The Rule of St. Benedict*, Chapter 58). Amidst our very busy schedules, we often overlook the potential impact of reading spiritual writings of the saints as a part of our daily lives.

Take up St. Benedict's challenge. Don't forget to make time for personal, fruitful reading. Your day will always be busy, whether with housework, grading papers, lesson planning, or running children to the next soccer practice or event. Amidst this chaos it is important to seek the guidance and inspiration of others, especially from the spiritual writings of the saints.

Don't be intimidated by reading the original works of the saints. Once you give their words a try, you will find that what they have written is much less complicated than you really think. Just because something was written many centuries ago, it does not mean it is not relevant to our lives today. Remember that God speaks to us in many different ways. He instructs us with more than just lectures and lessons. The words written by the great saints have survived because they have the power to inspire us.

## Exercise: Read the Writings of a Saint

The first task for today's exercise is to choose something to read. With so many saints to choose from, where do you start? Consider the following ways to choose a particular saint's spiritual writing:

- Flip through the *Catechism of the Catholic Church* and look through the footnotes for references from saints on a topic that appeals to you.

- Look at a Catholic calendar or search online for the "saint of the day."

- Ask your family or friends to recommend a favorite saint via social media.

- Search online for a list of the "Doctors of the Catholic Church" and start with one of their writings freely available online.

- Look through the books listed in a catalog or website of a Catholic book publisher.

- Pick a topic you will teach about in the coming days or weeks. Search online for the topic and include the name of a saint to find his or her writings about the topic.

If you are still undecided on what to read, you may want to choose a few passages from one of the most prolific Catholic writers and teachers of all time, St. Augustine of Hippo. Many of his works are freely available online, and most of them are broken up into short, consumable chapters that can be read in short bursts. If you have trouble finding one of his works to read, consider one of the following: *Confessions; City of God; Handbook on Faith, Hope, and Love;* or *A Sermon to Catechumens on the Creed.* All of these works should be freely available online or in many editions in book form.

When reading the writings of a great saint, the goal is not finishing for the sake of finishing. If there is a passage or a quote that really jumps out at you and inspires you, stop and think about it. Embrace what you have just read rather than racing through to finish it. Words or phrases from a saint's writing that inspire you will often find their way into the classroom.

As a disciple-teacher, we have so much to learn from the great saints and writers of the Church. Taking the time daily for spiritual reading just as St. Benedict suggested, can have a powerful impact on the way we teach as well as the way we live. By reading the advice of the saints and taking the way they lived their lives as models for our own, we become better disciples of Christ. Reading their words helps us to take on a new mindset, one that is oriented toward God and humbly accepts his will for our work as religious educators.

## Going Deeper

The writings of St. Paul in the letters of the New Testament have always been a very important resource for the great saintly writers throughout the Church's history. Pick a chapter out of one of Paul's letters and read it today for your own spiritual growth.

# Day 6

# Learn Something from Your Students

*"Amen, I say to you, unless you turn and become like children, you will not enter the kingdom of heaven. Whoever humbles himself like this child is the greatest in the kingdom of heaven." (Mt 18:3–4)*

During these first few days of this thirty-one-day journey we have focused on becoming a true disciple before we can become a true teacher. We have looked for lessons from Christ (Day 2), from a favorite teacher (Day 3), from the Bible (Day 4), and from the saints (Day 5). Today we will look for lessons we can learn from our students.

As disciples, sometimes we learn lessons in the places we least expect. Jesus definitely thought of children as one of the great sources of inspiration. He mentioned children as positive examples of discipleship, challenging his own followers to humble themselves like children in order to become the greatest in the Kingdom of Heaven.

The lessons we can learn from our students are often more subtle than from other sources. In order to learn from our students, we need to carefully observe and then deeply reflect on the lessons (both good and bad) that they can teach us. Children can remind us of God's gifts of innocence, beauty, awe, and inspiration, to name only a few.

Why is this so important? Just before his passion and death, Jesus asked to wash his disciples' feet. "You will never wash my feet," Peter said to him, but Jesus did it anyway (Jn 13:8). Jesus completely reversed the roles in this relationship. Through this great act of humility, Jesus provides all teachers an example to follow. *Be humble.* See your students in the loving way that God our Creator sees them.

This lesson of learning from our students is important in our roles as both disciples and servants. Later in this journey we will begin to focus on becoming servant-leaders, something Jesus showed us to do with the way he lived his life, but today we will focus on our students and the lessons we can learn from them.

## Exercise: Become Like One of Your Students

Consciously observe your students and other children today in order to see God's goodness in them. How can you be more like them in their innocence and wonder?

Keep Christ's words to "become like children" in the back of your mind by humbling yourself:

- How do these students relate to one another?
- What acts of kindness do I notice in their relationships?
- How do they share the bonds of friendship?
- How do they respond to you as a teacher?
- What kind of help do they seek from you?
- How do you appreciate their gift of humility?

Also, watch them at play. Answer for yourself:

- How do they show some kind of creativity, whether on the playground, at recess, at practices, in class, in their writing, in their doodling, in their singing?
- What do you think inspires this creativity and joy?

Finally, apply more of the lessons you have learned to your own life:

- How can you become more like them?
- What areas of your life do you need to approach anew as a child?
- In what areas of your life do you need help from others just as a child seeks help from you?

- How can you relate to God in the way your students related to one another?

- There may not be a moment of divine inspiration coming from one of your students today. Do not worry if you don't notice God's grace in some profound moment. Trust that God will help you remember how your students acted, and let those events lead you to reflect upon your own life and relationship with him. You can also ask for his help in reflecting on the events of the past few days or weeks to gain the inspiration for today's exercise. The key is to hone in on the details of your students' lives, taking the time to notice things you might typically take for granted.

Allow your students to teach you how to be a better disciple.

## Going Deeper

Think back to the days when you were a child. What were your dreams and aspirations? What kinds of things did you like to play and do? What are some of your fondest memories of childhood? Consider your life now. How can you find those same feelings of carefree joy and passion in your life today?

# Day 7

# Improve One
# Prayer Habit

*"Martha, Martha, you are anxious and worried about many things. There is need of only one thing. Mary has chosen the better part and it will not be taken from her." (Lk 10:41–42)*

Most teachers I know are Marthas. We have so much to do and so little time. With papers to grade, lessons to plan, worksheets to create, crafts to prepare, and meetings to attend, how can we possibly have time to pray? The good news is that in spite of all the stress, most teachers and catechists have a persistent feeling that they should be praying more.

I am no different from the teachers and catechists that I am describing, in fact, I'm probably worse. You would think that someone who is a regular teacher in his parish religious education program and who is writing a book on religious education would remember to pray. Like most

people, I forget to pray too. I have intense
success during liturgical seasons like Lent
fall short as time goes on.

Not long ago I decided to make prayer a      part
of my daily routine. But, like Martha, I was worried about
my time. I was anxious about the work that had to get
done at home and in the office. At the same time I craved
the devotion of Martha's sister, Mary. I knew that it was
important to start small and grow from there.

## Exercise: Make Prayer a Habit

Today's exercise is inspired by the lessons I learned in estab-
lishing prayer as a daily habit. These practices can be incorporated into your own prayer life.

**Write a sample of your daily routines from begin-
ning to end.** For example, when you wake up, do you
immediately hop in the shower or do you go brew a pot
of coffee? What routines do you have during lunchtime?
Before going to bed, do you grab a glass of water? What
is your tooth-brushing routine? Write all these routines
down in detail.

**Review your list and focus on one part of your day.**
When are some other opportunities for prayer? Usually
the best times to add extra prayer into your daily routine
are the times with the least amount of distractions, like

the early morning or late at night. Start small and grow from there.

**Pinpoint a trigger for prayer and rewrite your routine.** When I went through this exercise, I wrote down every detail of my morning, from coffee brewing to pouring my bowl of cereal. I rewrote my morning routine and decided to make coffee my *trigger*. Habits are triggered by other habits, our environment, and the people around us. I used brewing a cup of coffee as my trigger so that I would remember to pray right after I started the coffee maker. What action, habit, or place could you use as a trigger to pray?

**Research says it takes twenty-one days to form a habit.** Post your rewritten routine at the place where you have decided to pray and track your progress for twenty-one days. At the end of that time, your prayer habit should be so well ingrained as a part of your routine that you will feel awkward when you forget to pray.

**Habits always become stronger with support.** Tell your friends or loved ones that you are adding prayer to a specific part of your day. Invite them to join you or just ask them to pray for you as you make this change in your life. Be bold and share your experience with prayer on social networking sites or a blog. A public commitment is usually harder to break.

**Grace is required.** Do not try to develop a prayer life through hard work alone. Prayer is not just another task in your day. Sometimes we have to truly let go of our Martha-ness and just spend some unstructured, unplanned time with God. Depend on God to make your prayer habit work.

## Going Deeper

Have you added prayer to a particular time in your day? Now add one more occasion for prayer. Prayer does not have to be a once-per-day occurrence. Integrate prayer into a variety of times and places throughout your day. Make your prayer short, simple, and highly relevant to what you are doing at any particular time. Don't forget this simple definition: Prayer is talking to God!

# Part II

# **Become a Better Servant**

# Day 8

# Identify Your Students' Top Needs

*"[The Lord] guides the humble rightly,
and teaches the humble the way." (Ps 25:9)*

Recognizing and addressing the real needs of our students is a choice we all need to make. Teaching is not about our presentation and us, it is about the students and their participation. The more we focus on what our students need to *learn* rather than what we want to *teach*, the more success we will have in the classroom.

Think about the way Jesus taught and served the people. He did not wait for them to come to him (though they certainly did seek him out). He went out to them and visited them in their homes and shared meals with them. He recognized what was truly on their minds and addressed these things directly.

In a similar way, we need to uncover the greatest needs of our students and address them directly by meeting them where they are. This means we should focus our efforts less on our curriculum and lesson plans and more on the environment in which our students are learning or the ways in which they learn the best. This is true in all spheres of education—math, science, language arts, and the like—but especially in religious education.

In educational circles today, a popular term for our identifying and meeting our students' learning styles is "differentiated instruction." Teachers who use differentiation provide a variety of ways to teach that match up with the variety of ways students learn best and the various levels of understanding that each student has reached in a given lesson. Doing so requires a teacher to identify how students learn most effectively and then create activities that match up with those learning avenues.

At the core of this philosophy is a shift from teacher-centered classrooms to student-centered classrooms. Differentiated instruction includes several different kinds of learning methods. Sometimes more than one method will be employed in the same lesson.

## Exercise: Identify the Best Ways Your Students Learn

An understanding of how your students learn best will come to you over time as long as you are careful to observe

which learning styles are most successful
oping a full understanding of student le
multiple types of activities and see whicl
connect with the most. You can do the following:

**Survey your students.** One way to understand how
your students learn best is to ask them. Give your students
a list of several types of learning styles (for example, listening, speaking, reading, writing, viewing pictures, drawing
pictures, viewing videos, movement, music, interpersonal
group work, and intrapersonal reflection) with the following prompt: *Which of the following helps you learn and
understand new ideas the best? Choose the top three.* (See
www.thereligiointeacher.com/31days/day8 for a sample
survey.) Or you might just ask them to rank which ones
they like to do the most in class or outside of it. The results
will be a helpful insight to you as well.

**Spend one-on-one time with a student.** An even better way to identify your students' needs is to spend some
time teaching them one-on-one. While the rest of the class
is working on an activity, make a point of working with the
students who need your help the most. Keep in mind how
they respond to the questions you ask or the explanations
they understand the best. We will spend more time on this
during Day 10.

**Evaluate your next lesson plan.** Once you understand the different learning styles that are most effective with your students, make sure you are offering multiple types of learning during class time. Your students are going to be stronger in some areas than others. Likewise, you as a teacher are going to tend toward certain types of learning. Personally, I am a visual learner so I tend to use pictures, charts, and diagrams through lectures or videos while I teach. Other teachers and catechists like to use music and movement in the classroom. Still others like to guide students through intrapersonal meditation or creative writing. A challenge is to focus on the types of learning that connect best with your students rather than only yourself.

**Provide multiple variations on an activity.** Similarly, instead of providing just one way of doing an activity, provide students with multiple ways to get the same result. Try this approach with an activity or exercise from your next lesson. For example, if students are assigned to answer a question in a textbook, give them the opportunity to write out a response, but also allow them to draw a picture, share a response verbally with a partner, or work in a small group. Take note of what each student chooses to do and adjust your teaching moving forward to tend toward the strategies that work best for each person.

## Going Deeper

Different learning styles can also be applied to prayer. In what types of prayer do your students seem to best connect with God? Is it reading the Bible, journaling, meditating on icons, video meditations, prayer hand motions, music, group prayer circles, or some other form of prayer? Plan multiple types of prayer this year and take note of the ones your students like the best. At the same time, consider the types of prayer that fit best with your own personality. As a way to enter deeper into your own faith today, focus on the prayer practices that match up best with your personality in your personal prayer time.

# Day 9

# Identify Your Students' Biggest Strengths

*"Since we have gifts that differ according to the grace given to us, let us exercise them." (Rom 12:6)*

Now that we have identified our students' greatest needs and learning styles, let us turn to their greatest strengths. If you know where each student is strongest, you can help to cultivate those strengths into the passion that could one day drive them to pursue their own calling.

Unfortunately, our traditional education system is structured to ignore students' strengths. For example, standardized testing sends the message that all students are expected to perform equally well in all subjects and in all skills. The Catholic perspective on the human person, however, focuses on the unique gifts that each person brings into the world. As Catholic educators, we need to think of our classes as collections of individuals with individual strengths that contribute to the larger whole.

You should encourage diversity of interests and strengths within your classroom. This is the path of sanctity, which is different for everyone. C. S. Lewis fittingly contrasted the saints to tyrants in this way: "How monotonously alike all the great tyrants and conquerors have been: how gloriously different are the saints." Spend time encouraging students to grow in their strengths, so they can find their own path of sanctity.

## Exercise: Identify Your Students' Biggest Strengths

Never forget that every student in your class is made uniquely in the eyes of God. Every student is developing his or her own unique strengths, charisms, and passions, even at an early age. How do you recognize these unique gifts as a teacher?

**Start with their interests.** Human beings enjoy doing what we are good at and doing what we enjoy. Many young children, for example, love playing video games both because they are fun and because children are typically much more competent at the games than older people are, including their parents! With the nearly infinite number of levels and points that can be earned, it is easy for a child to feel a sense of accomplishment when playing a video game. Try to get a sense for your students' interests by ask-ing them to list what they like to do in their free time. The experience of play (free time), even for teenagers, is a great indicator of strengths and interests.

**Interpret the results.** Once we know what our stu-dents are interested in, how do we know what strengths we can help cultivate? First, let's clearly identify the kinds of strengths we are talking about. In a broad sense, students can be strong in skills that are interpersonal, intrapersonal, linguistic, logical, mathematical, analytical, visual, verbal, spatial, or naturalistic. More specifically, some students might be better at reading for comprehension than oth-ers. Others might like to play sports because they love the physical energy they expend. Other students might be bet-ter at puzzles than others. Some students might be bet-ter at visually showing ideas through artwork than others. Categorize their interests into types of strengths.

**Cultivate their strengths.** You will notice that most of the activities in this section of the book do not focus specifically on what we do in the classroom or what stu-dents actually learn. Remember, the focus should be on the students and their needs, not on creating a "perfect" lesson that might only meet the needs of a few. Therefore, you should take some time to cultivate your students' strengths even when these strengths seem to have nothing to do with religious education. If you spend some time in the coming days to help your students become better football players or singers by engaging in conversations with them about these strengths, then you have recognized and appreciated their unique skills and them as children of God.

At the same time, give students more time in class to execute their strengths in reference to learning. Based on your understanding of their strengths, allow students ownership over certain learning tasks (Day 19). For example, rather than expecting each student to learn something effectively by reading and showing what they have learned by writing, give them various opportunities to learn and be assessed based on their strengths. It might require more time on your part to develop these options, but this is why becoming a servant-leader is so important for your growth as a religious educator.

## Going Deeper

What are *your* greatest strengths? In addition to knowing your students' strengths and adjusting the way you teach, it is important to know your own personal strengths. You will be a more effective teacher when you teach from your strength areas. Identify your interests and strength areas, and consider how you can apply these to both planning and implementing effective lessons and managing a warm and caring classroom.

# Day 10

# Get to Know a Student before or after Class

*"I no longer call you slaves, because a slave does not know what his master is doing. I have called you friends, because I have told you everything I have heard from my Father." (Jn 15:15)*

One famous truth is especially applicable for teachers: "Nobody cares how much you know, until they know how much you care." No matter how much we know about the content of the lessons we teach, our students are less likely to listen if they think we do not care about them and their needs.

Think about how this was true in your own experience as a student. Your most memorable teachers were likely those who cared personally for you. You may not have even liked the subject they taught. As long as they cared personally about you, you considered them a good teacher. In the film *Mr. Holland's Opus*, talented musician

Glenn Holland (Richard Dreyfuss) despises teaching and his struggling music students because he sees himself as a composer, not a teacher. But when he starts to spend time teaching them one-on-one to help them improve, he clearly becomes proud of the growth he was able to cultivate in his students. The personal connection he makes with his students is the turning point in his teaching career.

A personal connection is especially important for students who act out with poor behavior. In many cases students who misbehave are starving for the attention of their peers and of their teachers. When they are given that attention in productive ways, they start to behave better in class and even start to listen during a lesson.

There is, however, a fine line to be drawn. Teachers and catechists have to be careful to keep a level of professionalism and not let an inappropriate friendship grow between them and their students. Students can misinterpret a relationship and start to expect special treatment. When you do have to discipline students, you don't want to hear, "But I thought we were friends!" Be on the lookout for this kind of misinterpretation or misunderstanding.

There are students in our classes who desperately need us. These are the students who consistently feel self-conscious and lack self-confidence. They need an adult figure to build them up. All students need some special attention in a given day. Maybe they had a rough night at home. They might have been made fun of by another kid at school. They could have failed a recent test. The list goes on and on.

## Exercise: Get to Know a Student Before or After Class

Today's exercise is simple one, but easy to overlook: get to know a student outside the routine of the day's lesson. How is this done? As a general rule, make sure it is possible to be in the classroom before students arrive and to be available in the room or in the hallway after class is over. Use the following tips to get to know your students better:

**Talk to a student before class begins or after class ends.** As the students enter the room, walk up to one of their desks and start a conversation. Or, stand at the entrance to the classroom to greet students and welcome them as they walk in. Starting conversations here is great as long as other students are able to enter the classroom as well! If time permits and parents are not waiting to pick up the students or they are not in a hurry to beat the bell to the next class, start a conversation with a student after class. Stay away from questions that could be quickly answered with a "yes" or "no." Ask open-ended questions to spark a conversation. It doesn't have to be a long or in-depth discussion, but a quick open-ended question is a great way to show that you care.

**Focus on something personal.** Start by discussing the activities that they participate in after school, like sports or clubs. If they have a book in hand, ask them to talk about it. If it is near the weekend, ask what they will be doing or what they did. Keep the questions general. Older teens, especially, will think you are prying if you get too specific. Try to stay away from the topic of class lessons and focus on their personal lives. Show the students that you genuinely care about them as people, not only as names on your class list.

**Select specific students.** Sometimes it can be convenient just to talk to the students who arrive to class early or tend to leave later than the others. This is important, but be sure to make an effort to talk to students who normally would not be around before or after class. Occasionally, ask to briefly meet a specific student after class. Share questions like those mentioned earlier, but make sure the student knows that he or she is not in trouble.

**What if there is no class today?** Depending on the day that you do this exercise, you may not see any students.

If this is the case, spend some time writin
email to one or two students that starts a
help you get to know them better (more
11). Just be sure to follow up with the student once you
see them in class to engage in a face-to-face conversation.

## Going Deeper

Read and reflect on a time that Jesus went out of his way
to get to know those who sought to learn from him. Start
with these two stories of Jesus visiting the houses of tax
collectors: Matthew the tax collector (Mt 9:9–13) and Zacchaeus the tax collector (Lk 19:1–10).

# Day 11

# Write a Note of Praise to a Student Who Struggles

*"Let another praise you—not your own mouth; some-one else—not your own lips." (Prv 27:2)*

Everyone likes to get a compliment, but no one needs positive reinforcement more than students who struggle. For many students, it is exactly this praise that will make all the difference in their lives many years down the road. The impact of well-placed praise for a student has been borne out in several studies by educational psychologists. For example, psychologist Carol Dweck believes that successful people maintain a "growth mindset"—that is, they believe their talents and intelligence are something that are cultivated and developed with time and effort. This is opposite from a "fixed mindset"—the belief that our intelligence is fixed and unable to grow.

Dweck goes on to suggest that we focus on the process and a person's efforts rather than abilities and outcomes as often as possible. In other words, we should praise children for their growth and progress, not where they may end up. Why is this important? According to Dweck's research, the more a student develops a growth mindset, the more likely he or she is to overcome failures and see them as only temporary defeats and opportunities for improvement.

Think about the students who lack self-confidence. They are mentally and emotionally beaten down by failures. They feel that each new mistake only piles on to their already growing list of failures. They need some positive reinforcement. They need to recognize that their intelligence, social skills, and even their physical abilities can grow over time. The students who struggle the most need the most praise to develop the confidence and competence they need to make these improvements.

In fact, God sees us with a growth mindset. We strive to do the good, but fail time after time. Our God is merciful and loving. He gives us the Sacrament of Reconciliation to help us recognize our failure and see it as an opportunity for growth. He gives us the grace to turn back to him again and again and do his will.

# Exercise: Write a Note of Praise to a Student Who Struggles

In a society that becomes more and more digitized every day, we tend to overlook the power of a hand-written note. Consider using one of the following formats and implement the suggestions that follow:

- thank-you cards

- customized stationery

- slips of paper designed especially for compliments

**Always have materials on hand.** Buy or create some special cards or slips of paper to write out notes of praise. If you buy some special cards or paper, or if you spend some time designing and creating blank notes, you are much more likely to follow through with this exercise. If you do not have the materials ready, you will not remember to write the notes!

**Choose a student or two who needs some praise the most.** Which students in your class need the biggest confidence boost? Who seems to be having a particularly bad day today? Who has shown signs of a dip in performance? Who have you not personally spoken to before or after class recently?

**Write the note.** Do not forget Carol Dweck's research: praise the effort, not the outcome. A student who volunteers for class discussion and politely raises his or her hand is a good example of praising effort, not an outcome. Many students have a fear of raising their hands. They fear failure and humiliation no matter how small. If you call on a student who has the wrong answer, it can be a great opportunity to praise him for putting himself out there and trying. When providing praise in writing, try to keep it short. You do not have to write a long note to get your point across. For younger children, stickers and fun designs can go a long way to get your point across.

**Give the student the note.** You can either give the student the note while they are working on an assignment in class or hand it to them on their way out of the class. This means you will need to take a few minutes of class time while students are working in groups or on their own to write the note. You could also write the note and give it to the student the next day, but the praise will be less powerful if behavior isn't fresh in his or her memory. Be subtle and do not draw attention to the gift. You do not want other students to be jealous or to draw unnecessary, embarrassing attention to the student you are trying to praise. It is okay to follow up with the student as well and share some additional verbal praise to support the note.

## Going Deeper

In your personal prayer time, do you spend enough time *praising* God? Praise is the form of prayer that "recognizes most immediately that God is God. It lauds God for his own sake and gives him glory, quite beyond what he does, but simply because he is" (*CCC*, 2639). In your own personal prayer time today, rather than petitioning God for something, simply offer praise. Most of us are not used to offering praise as a form of prayer, but it is powerful. It "embraces the other forms of prayer and carries them toward him" (*CCC*, 2639). If you need help getting started, consider praying with some Psalms of praise, especially Psalms 95, 96, 145, or 146.

# Day 12

# Compliment a Parent about Their Child

*"Hear, my son, your father's instruction,*
*and reject not your mother's teaching. . . ." (Prv 1:8)*

Parents have the most essential role in the education of their children. They are "the most influential agents of catechesis for their children" (*NDC*, p. 234). For this reason, it is absolutely necessary to involve parents in various aspects of our religious education programs.

One simple way to do this is to write parents (or guardians) a personalized note specifically about their child. Many catechists and teachers send out general notes to the class in the form of newsletters, folders, and packets. This is a great method of communication. At the same time, adding a personal element of communication can go a long way, whether it is a written note, an email, or a phone call. You might even write a brief, personalized note on the general update itself.

Similar to the way we praised the children (Day 11), be sure to direct the parents' attention to their children's effort rather than the outcomes of their work. Parents see the grades and they see some of the crafts and worksheets their children complete, but they do not know the whole story of how their son or daughter works and behaves in class. The most important information you can share is how their children are cooperating with others in class and where they are putting in the most effort.

## Exercise: Reach Out to a Parent or Guardian to Compliment a Child

As with offering praise to students, communication with parents about the success of their children in giving good effort should be undertaken on a regular basis. There are several ways to do this. Here are a few suggestions:

**First, choose a particular student who has made a positive effect on you or the other students.** Maybe the student made a thoughtful comment in class or shared something personal with you or the rest of the group. Maybe he or she showed an act of selfless assistance to a classmate that was not called for. Maybe a student who talks out often in class showed real effort to raise her hand today. Whatever the reason, be sure you have something specific to share with the parent.

**Next, consider the best method of communication.** Choose a method that may be more uncomfortable for you and require more effort, as these usually are more effective. Email, for example, is easy to send but hard to know if it is received. Written notes are powerful, but they often get lost in transit. Phone calls and one-on-one communication are more effective with parents because you will know that they will receive the compliment. Most of the time, parents get phone calls from teachers when the students are misbehaving. Getting a phone call with good news about something their children did can be surprising and much more memorable than the phone calls about misbehavior. Surprise parents with a phone call!

**What should you say?** Consider using the following template during your conversation (downloadable at www.thereligionteacher.com/31days/day12):

> Hi [parent's name], this is [student's name]'s [religion teacher/catechist]. I'm calling with some good news about your [son/daughter]. I want to share with you how impressed I have been with [his/her] actions. [He/she] [explain the positive actions or efforts you would like to share with the parent].
>
> These kinds of actions have made [him/her] an important asset to our classroom and [school/

parish] community. Thanks for everything you do
for [him/her].

I am always available if you have any questions
about your child's progress or if you want to hear
more about what we are doing in class. Just reach
out to me via [state how you would like parents
to contact you: e-mail, phone, written note, etc.].

Thanks for your time! Have a wonderful night.

Make sure to praise the student for a specific action or
effort rather than simply telling the parents they are raising
"a good kid." The specifics are important and should reinforce the goals you have for your students in the classroom.

Reach out to contact parents periodically throughout
the year to make this a habit. Do not wait for parent-
teacher conferences, open houses, or sacramental preparation meetings to speak personally with the parents.
Everyone is busy, and it can be a challenge, but the impact
of this communication can go a long way. Make it a goal
to contact one parent each week via phone or, if absolutely
necessary, email.

## Going Deeper

Take a few moments to think about your own parents or
those who have raised you. What role have they played in

your catechetical development? What are some specific ways they have positively impacted you and your faith in God? Say a prayer of thanksgiving for their impact on you or give them a call to say hello and thank them for being your parent.

# Day 13

# **Pray for Your Students**

---

*"And this is my prayer: that your love may increase ever more and more in knowledge and every kind of perception, to discern what is of value, so that you may be pure and blameless for the day of Christ." (Phil 1:9–10)*

Intercession is a powerful form of prayer. Jesus constantly prayed to the Father for other people's benefit. "Father, forgive them, they know not what they do," he prayed on the cross (Lk 23:34). At the Last Supper, he prayed to the Father for his disciples: "Keep them in your name that you have given me, so that they may be one just as we are" (Jn 17:11).

Praying for others is so important that Jesus instructed us to "love your enemies, and pray for those who persecute you" (Mt 5:45). This is why it is so important to pray for our students, especially on the days that we feel inconvenienced by their behavior or flat out angry at the way they acted. They need our prayers, and we need to be transformed by the act of praying.

Praying for your students is one of the best ways to truly serve them. You probably already do this, or at least you plan to do this as much as possible. Today you will prepare to pray for your students in a special way, in the way that they need it most.

## Exercise: Pray for Your Students

A common element of the exercises in part II devoted to helping you become a better servant is that they focus on specific, individual students rather than a group of students. Mother Teresa once said, "If you can't feed a hundred people, feed just one." She also said, "Never worry about numbers. Help one person at a time and always start with the person nearest you." Although we are responsible for an entire class or classes of students, we serve individual persons, not groups. In the same way, it is important that you pray for individual students rather than groups or classes as a whole. Consider these tips when praying for your students:

**Be sure you pray for all of them individually.** Find a class list or seating chart and pray for the entire class one by one as you read over the names. Make sure you have a complete list and check off each student as you pray for him or her. If you plan to spend a lot of time in prayer or if you have many students, feel free to spread out the prayers over the course of several days.

**Focus on the needs and the process, not the results.** When we pray for others, we pray for their needs, not necessarily the outcomes we hope to see. We have a tendency in all prayer to seek results, to seek answers to our problems. To take some more advice from Mother Teresa: "The success of love is in the loving—it is not in the result of loving." Focus on the needs of the individual students when you pray and ask only for the most important outcome our students can experience: the presence of God.

**Ask for help in your intercession.** Our devotion to the saints is another form of intercessory prayer. We pray to the saints so they will pray to God on our behalf and on the behalf of others. Ask for the saints to intercede on behalf of each of your students. If you have a particular devotion to a saint, ask for his or her intercession. You might even use the names of your students to call on particular saints to intercede for them. By default, turn to Mary for her intercession on the behalf of your students.

**Close with an Our Father.** Why the Lord's Prayer? If you notice when Jesus talks about prayer in the Gospels, he does not talk about an impersonal God. He prays to

"Our Father," not to "My Father," indicating that it is a shared relationship. This is a powerful aspect of the prayer he taught us. We ask for God's help as a Father, which makes us all his sons and daughters.

## Going Deeper

Why stop with your students? Pray for others in your life, especially those who challenge you the most. It may be a colleague or it may be just an acquaintance. Pray for individuals who need your prayers and especially for those for whom you have promised to pray.

# Part III

# **Become a Better Leader**

# Day 14

# **Eliminate the Time-Wasters**

*"I glorified you on earth by accomplishing the work that you gave me to do." (Jn 17:4)*

Religious education can be stressful for teachers and catechists. So much of this stress stems from the overwhelming amount of material that needs to be covered. The book or curriculum we receive at the beginning of the year seems overwhelming. There is just too much information! For religion teachers, the pile of papers to read, correct, and grade seems almost insurmountable. Volunteer catechists only have one short meeting per week with their students. How can they be expected to cover so much information?

The solution comes down to time management. Many teachers would be surprised by how much time is wasted during class. There are many little things that eat away at class time and take away from the valuable time that students could be spending learning in an engaged way. Here are the most common causes of lost time during class:

- Students are disruptive and talkative when class begins.

- Students pack up before class ends.

- Students waste time while transitioning from one activity to the next.

- Students do not understand the directions, so they choose to do nothing and rarely ask for help.

- Students take too long to turn in papers or forget to hand in their homework.

- Students interrupt class with questions about procedures (Day 15), like sharpening their pencils, going to the bathroom, or throwing something in the trash.

These are only some of the causes of a disorganized classroom. Focus your energy on setting up systems and procedures to ensure class time is used efficiently, and you will be able to get more done each period. This will help you to create a classroom environment where students are eager to learn.

# Exercise: Eliminate the Time-Wasters with These Proven Teaching Strategies

In order to get back that much-needed time in your class, implement some or all of these five proven strategies for managing a more efficient and effective classroom:

**1. Bell work.** Start each class session or day with bell work. Bell work is an activity or task that students complete immediately after they walk in the door. Write out the assignment on the board or have handouts or packets for students to pick up in a designated location as they enter the room. Doing bell work quiets students as they enter class, cuts down on the chatting when class begins, and sends a message to the students that this is a time for focused work.

**2. Repeat your instructions.** A lot of class time is lost because students are not exactly sure what they should be doing at any given time. When you introduce an activity to students, be sure to repeat yourself. Explain it in different ways until you are sure every student understands the directions. Ask one or two students to repeat back the instructions that you have given. Hearing the instructions in the words of their peers helps all of the students better understand. Plus, the possibility of being called on to repeat the instructions will give students a great reason to listen to instructions the first time. Repeating instructions is essential when transitioning students from one activity to the next.

**3. Automate answers to common questions.** As weeks go by, you will start to hear the same questions over and over again. Once this happens, create a procedure (Day 15) and teach it to students so that they all know the answer to the question before it comes up. For example, in a religion teacher's classroom the procedure for turning in homework should never be a question. Determine and announce a regular procedure and stick with it; for example, a box in the room to place homework or a regular routine at the beginning of class to pass homework to the front of a row. Whatever method you choose, be consistent and make sure every student knows how they should turn in their homework each class period.

**4. Advance organizers.** Advance organizers are a list of goals and activities that students will accomplish. They serve as an agenda or detailed schedule for what will happen in class. These agendas will answer the question on most students' minds when they come in: What are we doing today? During class, it will answer another common question: What are we doing next?

**5. Prioritize the content.** You will not be able to cover everything. All textbooks include more information than is possible to teach in a given year. Prioritize the most important lessons and simplify the messages (Day 23). Focus your class time on these priorities. If students do master the priorities you have set, then spend more time teaching the secondary lessons and material in their textbook or curriculum.

## Going Deeper

While efficiency is important for learning, we can get so caught up in getting things done that we do not take the necessary time to slow down and connect with God. Accomplishing a task is a short-term accomplishment. Spending time in prayer focuses on a long-term goal. Do not ignore the need for prayerful reflection both in your personal time and during class time. Time in prayer is time well spent no matter how much there is to do. Do not forget to set aside some time to pray today and refer back to Day 7 if some of your prayer habits need to be reestablished.

# Day 15

# Update Your Classroom Procedures

*"For lack of guidance a people falls." (Prv 12:14)*

Too many teachers focus only on their rules as the guiding force behind their classroom discipline and keeping their classrooms running smoothly. However, rules in and of themselves are never able to create a productive learning atmosphere on their own.

Classroom *procedures* are different from classroom *rules*. Procedures are the established set of routines and instructions that students follow out of habit. Procedures include things like sharpening a pencil, handing in home-work, and moving from one place to another. Unlike a classroom rule, breaking a classroom procedure does not initiate a consequence. Procedures answer questions that are frequently repeated on a daily or weekly basis, such as:

- Can I go to the bathroom?

- Can I sharpen my pencil?

- Can I throw this away?

- What do I do when I finish the assignment?

- What is today's homework assignment?

- Where do I put my finished assignment or homework?

- What are we doing today?

- What should I do when I arrive in class?

- Can I erase the board?

In an effectively run classroom, students follow procedures because they have been trained to do so. No punishment is needed. They know where to put their homework because they've been shown where it goes and put it there out of habit. Rules, on the other hand, point to positive behaviors students should embrace and negative behaviors they should avoid. When a rule is broken, there is a consequence, but when a procedure is forgotten or improperly carried out, the students are taught again.

## Exercise: Update Your Classroom Procedures

Consider the following suggestions for defining and implementing classroom procedures:

**Identify the issues.** Make a list of the most common and basic questions you get from your students. You can start with the preceding list if you wish. Next, list the instructions you find yourself repeating again and again. These are all issues that can be resolved by training the students in new procedures.

**Design new procedures.** List new procedures that address the questions and issues you just identified. First, write the details and then rewrite the procedures in more concise terms. Prepare for every misunderstanding or question that might arise from the procedure. If your procedure for sharpening pencils is to have it done before class, make sure you have a corollary for when a pencil breaks during class (i.e., have extra sharpened pencils at your desks, wait until the teacher finishes talking, etc.).

**Practice the procedures.** Since procedures are routines and performed by habit, they need to be practiced for them to work. Set aside some time during class to practice (not just explain) each new procedure. The best time for this to be done is at the beginning of a new school year. Practicing procedures is much more effective than giving students a written description of the procedures (though posting them on the wall or distributing a printout would not hurt!). It may take weeks for students to learn these new procedures, especially if they have to unlearn other procedures and habits in the meantime. In the long term, you will find this is time well spent.

**Tweak the procedures.** Hold on to your procedures until it is absolutely necessary to change one or more of them. If there are procedures that need to be adjusted, enlist the students' input and make a switch. The more they are involved in the decision, the more likely they are to remember the new procedure (see Day 19 on giving ownership to students). Practice each change and expect it to take a few weeks to be completely mastered.

**Correct students effectively.** The temptation is to establish a consequence when a procedure is ignored or overlooked. Remember these procedures are followed out of habit, so if students forget, they need to practice until it is learned by rote. Correct the students with constructive feedback (Day 18) and have them practice until they follow the routines out of habit, but do not initiate a punishment to teach them how to do the procedures. Don't forget: Procedures are not rules!

## Going Deeper

A lot of our Catholic prayer practices are done out of habit as well. Once we learn to make the Sign of the Cross or how to conduct ourselves during Mass, we are better able to focus on God when we pray and praise him. Consider some familiar routines for prayer and liturgy. Think about why these procedures were established. For example, what is the significance of genuflecting or bowing our heads in prayer? Why do we begin prayer with the Sign of the Cross? Why do we kneel during the eucharistic prayer? You may wish to spend some time researching the answers to any questions you are unsure of.

# Day 16

# Update Your Classroom Rules

*"The law of the LORD is perfect,
refreshing the soul." (Ps 19:8)*

The main difference between classroom rules and classroom procedures (Day 15) is that rules have consequences. If a student forgets the proper procedures for arriving to class and beginning the bell work assignment, then the procedure needs to be retaught. But if a student enters the class late or disruptively by interrupting other students who are trying to do their work, then consequences are needed to correct the poor choice.

The intended outcome for rules is the same as for procedures. In each case the goal is the same. We want our students to be focused on their work so they can learn more about their faith and become closer with the Lord. Rules help to protect the rights of all students to be able to reach these goals. Rules deal with respect. Their ultimate foundation is in Jesus' call to love our neighbor as another self.

Do not forget your role as a teacher or as a catechist. We are servant-leaders. We must serve the class by protecting those who follow the rules. We must enforce the rules for the benefit of both the students who obey them and those who break them. Anger is not part of the equation as we enforce consequences. We recognize that rules and consequences are the way to provide students extra help in loving their neighbor and themselves.

Today's lesson is applicable to one of the six fundamental tasks of catechesis according to the *General Directory for Catechesis*: moral formation. "This moral testimony, which is prepared for by catechesis, must always demonstrate the social consequences of the demands of the Gospel" (*General Directory for Catechesis*, 85). Crafting understandable and fair classroom rules and enforcing them consistently is much more effective in fostering moral development in young people than simply teaching *about* morality.

## Exercise: Update Your Classroom Rules

There are two possible activities in today's exercise. You can either rewrite your classroom rules or try new ways to communicate your current classroom rules to your students. Use the following guidelines to rewrite or better communicate your classroom rules:

**Clarity.** Are your classroom rules written in concise, easy-to-understand language? Does each rule clearly communicate the model behavior? "Show respect to your neighbor" sounds like a great rule, but it does not clearly communicate *how* to show respect. On the other hand, a rule like "show respect to your neighbor by keeping your hands to yourself" clearly indicates the behavior that would cause a consequence. If a rule leaves room for interpretation, you will find yourself arguing with students over their behavior. Be clear about the behaviors you want students to avoid.

**Positive.** It is tempting to frame all classroom rules like the Ten Commandments: "Thou shall not . . ." However, we want to create classroom rules that express correct behavior, not just misbehavior. If necessary, flip your rules to communicate a positive model for behavior. Instead of "do not talk out," state "raise your hand when you ask a question or want to add a constructive comment to the class." Instead of "do not get out of your seat without permission," state "raise your hand to ask for permission to leave your seat." The behavior you *want* students to show is contained in this positive communication of the rules rather than only the behavior you *do not* want them to show.

**Reminders.** Just like with classroom procedures, students need reminders of the rules. Review the classroom rules at least monthly. Post them on a bulletin board or poster board on the wall. Have students tape them inside of their textbooks, notebooks, desks, or binders.

**Consequences.** Communicating the consequences for rules is just as important as knowing the rules themselves. Consequences include any loss of special privileges, such as recess, lunch with friends, class games, free time after school, and participation in sports and other activities. Stay away from consequences that confuse learning with punishment. In other words, do not assign extra homework or additional assignments as a consequence, or you will send the message that all homework assignments and learning activities are always punishment. Teachers and catechists also typically allow one or two warnings before enforcing a consequence.

## Going Deeper

It is not very often that we welcome punishment in our own lives. When we sin, we tend to expect forgiveness out of God's great mercy. In addition to God's mercy, we need his justice. This is why the Sacrament of Reconciliation includes a penance. Like a consequence for breaking a rule, a penance helps us change for the better so the next time we are tempted by sin, we will have the ability to resist it. Take some time today to recognize some of your shortcomings and sins, and then think of a penitential act (prayer, service, giving something up) to help train yourself to avoid that behavior the next time.

# Day 17

# Articulate the Vision for Your Classroom

---

*"I came so that they might have life and have it more abundantly." (Jn 10:10)*

Now that you have firmly established the procedures and rules within your classroom, it is time to take the next step. Classrooms that include procedures and rules are essential, but teachers and catechists who hide behind their intended efficiency can easily fall into the trap of ignoring the big picture of *why* the procedures and rules were initiated in the first place. These kinds of teachers and catechists are looked at as authoritarian and eventually alienate their students due to a lack of unifying vision. If the only motivation for our students to follow procedures is because of their training, and rules from the fear of punishment, then we are likely to have a rebellion on our hands!

Great leaders unite their followers in a common vision. The most magnetic visions are simple, yet profound. They are exciting and motivating for people to rally around and work toward as a group. Think of John F. Kennedy's vision to put a man on the moon or Martin Luther King Jr.'s vision of America in his "I Have a Dream" speech. These leaders communicated a vision, and people followed.

What does it take to create a vision? For some teachers, this vision may already be established as part of a parish or school mission statement or charism. Sometimes this vision is displayed on posters in the halls or in student orientation. In this case, latch onto this vision and focus on the areas that connect best with your classroom. This will help you communicate a common classroom vision for your students because it will be backed up and reinforced in many other aspects of school or parish life.

What is the ultimate goal or outcome that you are working toward with your students? Always keep in mind the higher purpose your students will be pursuing if they indeed listen to and obey the rules. The answers may not be obvious, but they do not have to be profound. One year as a teacher, I focused on *respect* as the focal point of everything we did in class. I related all of the rules, procedures, and work we did in class to the idea of respect. Respect is not a really profound topic, but it was a start. I was able to come back to the concept again and again while teaching students certain behaviors and motivating them to learn.

# Exercise: Articulate the Vision for Your Classroom

Start to develop your vision by brainstorming a list of words and phrases that you personally believe in and passionately want to share through your teaching. For example, you might include a set of virtues on your list like humility, prudence, justice, temperance, fortitude, faith, hope, and love. Maybe you want to focus on the particular charisms of your parish's or school's namesake or founder. For example, a vision of becoming "men for others" could already be a part of your school's vision if you teach in a Jesuit all-boys school. Likewise, many Congregation of Holy Cross institutions focus on the phrase "make God known, loved, and served," which has its origin with the Holy Cross founder, Blessed Basil Moreau.

Next, refer to the exercise on Day 1 when you articulated your calling as a religious educator. This list is a great place to find some ideas for your classroom vision. Which word or words translate easily from your own deep-rooted calling to the vision you wish to share with your students?

Once you have selected a handful of words or phrases, start to do some free-writing or further brainstorming about how these virtues, charisms, or gifts have practical application to your students. Compare your list to your students' needs and strengths that you identified in Day 8 and Day 9. Also, how do these words relate to your procedures (Day 15) and rules (Day 16)? How do they relate to the themes and lessons in the topics in your textbook and course you are teaching this year?

Put your vision to a test. How can you introduce this vision to your students? How will your students understand it? Will you be able to convince just one student to get behind this vision? Will you be able to convince half of the class? Everyone?

Finally, decide how you will articulate this vision further. This is something you will have to do frequently. What are songs that personify this vision and would help explain its importance (see Day 27)? How can you summarize the vision in a few words that can be displayed prominently in the room? What symbols and themes can you use to remind students of the vision in the way that you design and decorate the room (desks, bulletin boards, nametags, inscribed at the bottom of tests and handouts, etc.)? Use these and other methods to constantly remind students of the reason your time together is so important.

## Going Deeper

Choose any New Testament letter of St. Paul. Read the opening introduction. What vision is Paul trying to rally people around in this letter? Next, read the conclusion of the letter. How does Paul restate his vision? What parts of St. Paul's vision can you pursue in your daily life at home, work, and in the classroom?

# Day 18

# Practice Giving Positive, Constructive Feedback

*"Encourage yourselves daily while it is still today."*
*(Heb 3:13)*

Offering positive and constructive feedback to your students is critical to their development. This type of feedback will include pointing out your students' mistakes. There is nothing wrong with this type of criticism as long as it is not meant to intentionally damage a student's self-confidence. This is what makes it *constructive* criticism. In fact, all criticism, it if it is to be constructive, must build up a student's self-confidence in order to produce growth.

On Day 11 the goal was to praise students for their effort and hard work by writing them a note. Today the focus is on how to correct mistakes by giving constructive feedback. Recall the research of educational psychologist Carol Dweck. Her hypothesis is that we all have two mindsets: a growth mindset, which accepts failure as an opportunity for growth, and a fixed mindset, which sees failure as an unavoidable consequence of intelligence (or skill, experience, genetics, etc.). The way we cultivate the growth mindset is helping students feel competent and able to overcome the mistakes they make in their work. The difference between writing a note of praise to a student (Day 11) and today's exercise is that today we are giving students constructive criticism that is meant to point out mistakes and provide an avenue for improvement.

Teachers and catechists are correct to use student work and tests as a place to offer feedback. Tests and other assignments are primarily meant to assess student learning, but they can also be a place to record a constructive comment. Letter grades and scores have a fixed quality to them that is hard to ignore. This exercise offers ways to go beyond negative markings on tests and a final grade to be able to offer further feedback.

A fixed mindset is not limited to a written grade. Imagine a fixed mindset in the area of faith. We certainly are not born with a deep-level understanding of the mystery of God. And, in fact, we will never uncover the depth and breadth of God completely. Nevertheless, we are called to deepen our faith and understanding. The only way we do that is to keep a growth mindset while also offering our students the constructive feedback necessary for them to do the same.

## Exercise: Give Positive, Constructive Feedback

Offering positive feedback and constructive criticism is not limited to writing detailed comments on a student's test or assignment. You should have several opportunities to carry out this exercise in the coming days in different ways. Consider giving positive and constructive feedback verbally to a student who falls short either behaviorally or academically. Of course, do continue to write constructive comments on your students' written work too. If you do not have any written work to correct, write a separate note to a student providing some constructive feedback about their behavior or effort in class. Use the following approaches to frame your feedback:

**The sandwich approach.** The classic framework for providing positive and constructive feedback is called the "sandwich approach." Start with a positive compliment about something the student did well, end with a word of positive encouragement, and provide some constructive criticism in the middle. Breaking the ice with the honest, positive compliment makes a big difference in shaping the mindset of a student so he or she can welcome the constructive criticism that comes in the middle as an opportunity to grow.

**Positive feedback.** When you provide positive feedback, it is important that this feedback be legitimately earned and task-specific. In other words, make it honest, believable, and concrete. Do not tell a student they did a nice job on an assignment when they missed the majority of the test items. Instead, point out the specific areas and tasks where they did well or showed improvement (think growth!). For example: "John, you are showing improvement in the way you sit up in your chair. A few weeks ago, you were slouching all the time, but now you are showing me you are engaged in the class." With positive feedback, help students to see a series of small wins so they can build up their confidence and ability to overcome the seemingly larger losses.

**Constructive criticism.** Just like the positive feedback, the constructive criticism should point out the specific task that caused the mistake and show a way to fix it. "Grading" an assignment with red marks all over it only helps you know how to add up a student's score. It does not necessarily help students understand their mistakes so they can fix them (again, think growth). When assessing student work, think of it as "correcting" rather than "grading." Instead of just marking an answer incorrect, point out the error and write something like, "see page 68, paragraph 3 for the correct answer." If these kinds of marks are too time-consuming, make sure you will dedicate the necessary time to reteach the commonly missed questions or give students the opportunity to relearn what they missed. Criticism is constructive when it builds upon mistakes from the ground up.

## Going Deeper

Think for a moment about how critical you are of yourself. Do you think of yourself with a fixed mindset or a growth mindset? Think about the last time you made a mistake. Do you think of that mistake as something unavoidably caused by your personality (fixed) or something that can be corrected (growth)? We are all called to be saints, and we all have the capacity for sanctity as long as we are willing to allow God's grace to come into our lives. Make a note today of three times in your life where you realized that with God nothing is impossible. How can those lessons help you overcome a current roadblock or mistake?

# Day 19

# Give Students Ownership over Certain Tasks

*"I no longer call you slaves, because a slave does not know what his master is doing." (Jn 15:15)*

Great leaders are not afraid of involving their followers in the process of pursuing their common goals. Great leaders appeal to the strengths of their followers and help them pursue the passion God has placed within their hearts. Giving students ownership means inviting them to be active participants in the goals and vision of the classroom (Day 18) rather than passive recipients of rules (Day 16) and procedures (Day 15).

To give students ownership means involving them in decisions about reaching class goals. This could include decisions about learning tasks, classroom procedures, and prayer. There are two main reasons why this is crucial to your success as a teacher or catechist.

First, giving students ownership appeals to the human desire for *self-determination*. This is a term used by educational psychologists Edward Deci and Richard Ryan to describe our desire for a sense of control over our lives and work. We are motivated to accomplish that which we are personally invested in completing. Imagine if, as a teacher, you had no control over *what* you taught your students and *how* you taught it. Imagine if every moment of your day was scripted. How would you feel with this complete loss of freedom? Similarly, this desire for freedom, which God has placed as an innate desire within the hearts of each one of us, is embraced when students are given ownership over their own learning experience.

Second, giving ownership to your students removes a burden from you. As teachers, we tend to try to do everything ourselves. Giving up complete control of our classroom is a very big challenge. Being a leader is not about being authoritarian; it is about being an authority. Making this shift toward increased student ownership allows you to take on the role of mentor and guide. The focus of the classroom is rightfully re-oriented toward the student rather than the teacher. This connects with our goals to become both servant-leaders and disciple-teachers.

In recent years this movement toward giving students greater ownership of their learning experience has become increasingly popular. The proliferation of computers and tablets in schools, along with better online educational resources, have allowed students to take more control over learning and become more able to solve problems and answer questions on their own than ever before. The concept of "flipping the classroom" has become a popular way to describe the shift from lecture-focused to work-focused class time. In reality, this should have always been our goal, with or without the help of technology. The more students have ownership over their learning experience, the more motivated they will be to learn about their faith.

## Exercise: Give Students Ownership

To embrace your students' desire for freedom and self-determination, begin by giving them ownership of at least one class task and one student learning activity. For example, all of the following special tasks could be assigned and rotated throughout the year:

- Clean the board

- Set up learning centers

- Update the calendar

- Deliver papers to the office

- Straighten the desks
- Select music for meditation
- Lead class prayer

Other regular jobs you might consider are "row leaders" or "group leaders," who are in charge of collecting papers from their rows or groups as well as straightening desks or even checking to make sure everyone has the necessary materials for a given project or task. Set up a way to assign all of these jobs. Give students the opportunity to rotate jobs on a weekly or biweekly basis, for example. All of these jobs will then become a part of your classroom procedures (Day 15).

For today's exercise, don't feel the need to revamp classroom methods you already have in place. Instead, choose one or two tasks that you normally do yourself and assign them to the students. If the new assignments work well, you may want to update your classroom procedures again to include this new way of doing things. In a couple of weeks, analyze how things have gone since you handed off some of the tasks. Ask the students for their input at that time as well.

We can also give students ownership over learning experiences. Doing so gives students more opportunities to embrace their strengths (Day 9) and address their greatest needs (Day 8). In the days ahead, we will focus on becoming a better teacher by setting goals and using a variety of teaching methods to reach those goals. As you go through the final section of daily exercises, think about other ways you can hand over ownership of class tasks and learning experiences to your students. All of the teaching strategies mentioned in the days ahead will be more effective when matched with student ownership.

## Going Deeper

God gives us ownership over our lives. We call this free will. At the same time he wishes to cooperate with us and help us to be co-creators with him. Reflect on your life and work. When do you feel the most free to achieve your goals? What sense of ownership in planning your lessons and leading your class have you been given? Thank God for the gift of ownership he has given you in these parts of your life and for his presence with you.

# Part IV

# **Become a Better Teacher**

# Day 20

# Write Out Why the Lesson Is Important

---

*"Woe to you, scribes and Pharisees, you hypocrites. You pay tithes of mint and dill and cummin, and have neglected the important things of the law: judgment and mercy and fidelity." (Mt 23:23)*

At some point in their lives every teacher will hear these words from their students: "Why do I have to learn this?" or "I will never use any of this information in my entire life." Most of the time teachers react in defensiveness or anger, accusing students of being naïve or even rude. If you ever get this question and the immediate response that comes to your mind is "Because I said so!" then pause, reflect, and take a moment to provide a real answer. "Why are we learning this?" is an honest question in need of an honest answer. In today's exercise we will identify why we believe the lessons we teach are important. By doing this, we will help students understand the *why* behind what they learn.

In fact, there is a sense from older students that the only classes that are really important are those that are necessary for college acceptance or that will connect with a future career or profession. This is really a sad effect of the productivity-focused society we live in. For religious education, this is an especially important issue, because religion courses are not required for college acceptance. This means religious educators have an even more daunting challenge in convincing their students why their class is important. When we make religion a personal and important part of the lives of our students, then we are on our way to achieving this goal.

On Day 8 we focused on uncovering our students' needs. Today you are going to focus on what students *want*—but do not necessarily need—from religious education. You will use this information to transform your lesson. Once you have a clear understanding of what your students find valuable, you will be able to passionately articulate benefits to learning that will grab your students' attention.

For example, imagine you are teaching a group of eighth graders about the gifts of the Holy Spirit. Motivating fourteen-year-olds is not easy. It is tempting to tell them that they have to learn something "because it is on the test." This answer is accurate, but it is not much more motivating than the standard "because I said so" response. Why? These reasons are primarily external to the lives of the students. The mention of a test invokes fear, and fear leads students to treat learning as a means to an end. When this is the case, even cheating makes a lot of sense to them. If students are only motivated to learn the gifts of the Holy Spirit to pass a test, then taking whatever means necessary to pass that test makes a lot of sense to them.

Instead, think of how the gifts of the Holy Spirit relate to a particular group of students' interests. For example, the gift of fortitude (courage) is very important to athletes. The gift of knowledge is a gift all students need to do well in school. The gift of counsel (right judgment) helps all people make good decisions when they are unsure of right and wrong. The gift of understanding will help two friends support each other in times of need.

These particular reasons are broad, but the purpose of today's exercise is to make connections like these that specifically appeal to your students. In order to do so, you must be keenly aware of your students' personal interests and the activities they participate in during their free time. If you have not done so already, have the students fill out a sheet of paper or note card listing their hobbies, sports, favorite movies, favorite books, and favorite school subjects. Also, make a greater effort to know your students personally outside of classes (Day 10). This is a good starting point for making the connection between a lesson and the students' interests.

## Exercise: Write Out Why a Lesson Is Important

For this exercise, have your lesson plan available for the next class you are scheduled to teach. Examine the topic and activities you have planned for that class. Consider the following in relation to your upcoming lesson:

**Answer the question for yourself: Why do I have to know this?** Or, how has knowing this information benefited *me*? For example, knowing more about how the Holy Spirit relates to God the Father and God the Son has completely transformed the way I understand who God is. Knowing the structure of Jesus' parables and some examples of them has made listening to the Gospel and homilies on Sunday much more interesting.

**List all the benefits of learning what you are teaching.** Write down every reason you can think of for knowing about this topic. The point here is to brainstorm and list as many ideas as possible. You will narrow the list soon. After you have listed your personal benefits, think of the benefits for other adults and then for students of many different ages. Write these down too.

**Highlight the benefits that would appeal the most to your group of students.** Think about your students and how they spend their free time (hobbies, sports, etc.), and consider how these interests align with the benefits you have listed. What benefits of learning about this topic would connect most with their interests and likes? How could they apply a particular prayer practice or spiritual lesson to their own personal lives?

**Select the hook for your lesson.** This is the crucial application of this day's exercise. Once you have determined the benefits that will be most appealing for your students, refer to those benefits as part of a lesson starter or hook, and continue to refer back to the benefits as you continue the lesson. If you can hook them at first with some things they are interested in, you will be able to reel them in to effectively learning the topic of the day. If students can make connections between their personal lives and the lessons they learn, you will have a much more engaged classroom.

In many cases you will find tasks and objectives that do not connect very well to a clear benefit. It is hard to justify how memorizing the definition of a vocabulary term is going to reap some serious benefit in anyone's personal life. However, memorizing a definition can be a great first step to a larger goal with a more relevant and exciting purpose. Connecting each gift of the Holy Spirit with practical needs and occasions in life will help students to not only remember the names of the seven gifts, but be able to call on them when they will be especially needed in their personal lives.

## Going Deeper

Pick a form of prayer that you practice fairly often, for example, the Rosary, stating intentions, reading Scripture, a novena, the Angelus, the Examen, the Stations of the Cross, the Liturgy of the Hours, or spontaneous prayer. Why is this form of prayer so important to you? Why do you pray this way, and why would someone else find value in this kind of spiritual growth in their lives? Write out the answers to these questions and spend some time practicing this prayer while keeping in mind the meaning that it has for you.

# Day 21

# **Draft or Edit Student Learning Objectives**

*"Just one thing: forgetting what lies behind but straining forward to what lies ahead, I continue my pursuit toward the goal, the prize of God's upward calling, in Christ Jesus." (Phil 3:13–14)*

One of the most often quoted habits in Steven Covey's popular book, *The 7 Habits of Highly Effective People*, is "begin with the end in mind." This is advice that teachers and catechists should take to heart. When educators plan a lesson, they tend to focus only on the activities, worksheets, lectures, and other tasks that fill up the time of the day. This is the wrong approach. When the focus is more on the activities students will do and not the intended outcomes, the following negative results can occur:

- Students may fail to see the purpose of what they are learning.

- Teachers and catechists can be unclear on what the students should know.

- Learning activities can turn into busy-work assigned just to pass the time.

I can remember one embarrassing moment during my first year as a religion teacher. My students were quietly answering questions on a worksheet when my principal came into the room and asked curiously, "What are they working on?" "Busy-work," I replied without thinking. Needless to say she was not happy with my response.

There is nothing wrong with using worksheets and handouts. I still use them often as a parish catechist. But it is important that any seatwork you assign has clear connections with the students' learning objectives for the lesson. Managing a productive group of students is important, but without goals, the work they do can lead in many different directions. All activities must have a meaningful purpose and engage students in a common goal. Every minute we spend in the classroom should be spent directing students to that goal.

In many ways, naming and recording student learning objectives are like entering an address into a global positioning system (GPS). The destination is clear, but the roads we take can change along the way. Do not be afraid to focus on the learning objective while remaining flexible to the "recalculating" that can occur while the lesson progresses. You can never really be sure which strategies will work the best to get your students to reach the objective, but having sight of a clear destination will help you adjust the lesson as you go along.

## Exercise: Draft or Edit Student Learning Objectives

A learning objective (or lesson objective) is a sentence that describes what you want the students to learn. It has three parts: the acronym SWBAT (see next), an action verb, and the topic of the lesson.

**1. SWBAT.** The form I like to use to frame student learning objectives is "SWBAT," which stands for "Students will be able to . . ." In other words, at the end of a lesson *students will be able to* illustrate that they have mastered the objective for the day. I do not like "Students will . . ." because teachers and catechists tend to list what the students *will do* during a lesson (activities, worksheets, projects, etc.) instead of what they *will be able to do* because of those activities.

**2. An action verb.** It is easy to come up with passive learning verbs like "learn" or "understand" as a part of the lesson objective. The problem with these types of verbs is that as a teacher it is difficult to measure "learning" or "understanding" as an action. Instead, action verbs indicate students doing something with the knowledge they have gained. In other words, students will be able to *list, recite, define, identify, describe how, describe why, build, categorize, compare and contrast, select the best way to, analyze*, etc. These verbs can easily be applied to some form of assessment to measure student progress toward the objective (Day 22).

**3. The topic of the lesson.** What is the actual topic of the lesson? This is where you will need to think hard about the most important concepts or skills you want the students to learn. It helps to write your list of main ideas as questions. Next, you can easily turn your list of questions into learning objectives. For example, "What are the names of the four Gospels?" would become "Students will be able to name (or list) the four Gospels."

Now that you have a better understanding of the three components of a learning objective, plan one of your upcoming lessons with these steps:

**1. Choose the topic.** Pick a topic (or topics) for an upcoming lesson. Start with your textbook and list the vocabulary words, main ideas, and review questions that the students will encounter as they read. Also, consult your school, parish, or diocesan standards for religious education for items and objectives that might pertain to this particular lesson.

**2. Brainstorm objectives.** List all of the questions the students should be able to answer by the end of the lesson. Next, turn those questions into objectives. You should include both easier and more difficult objectives.

**3. Select the most important objectives.** Many learning objectives build on one another to achieve a much more complex objective. Select the highest-level objective or objectives and write those at the top of your lesson plan.

While you teach the lesson, you will want to keep these objectives handy to remind you that they are the foundation of everything your students do. Write them on the board so the students know and remember why they are doing the tasks that you assign. Write them on a Post-it note or keep your lesson plan in front of you at all times. If you get off track, if an activity you have planned is not helping the students reach the objective, or if you are running out of time, you can change course and try something else to help them meet the goals you have set as the learning objectives.

On Day 22 we will focus on assessment, but until then keep in mind that you will want to establish some way of checking up on students to be sure each of them (not just the class as a whole) is able to illustrate mastery of the objective. Always plan some kind of check-up to see if students have mastered the objective of the lesson.

## Going Deeper

The *Catechism of the Catholic Church* states that "the Beatitudes reveal the goal of human existence, the ultimate end of human acts: God calls us to his own beatitude" (*CCC*, 1719). Read the Beatitudes (Mt 5:3–11) and choose one that you could especially work toward today. At the end of the day assess your progress toward living this beatitude.

# Day 22

# Assess Without a Test

*"Test everything; retain what is good." (1 Thes 5:21)*

In the previous day we set meaningful learning objectives to direct student activities, worksheets, projects, and other teaching strategies. Today we will focus on ways you can check to make sure each student is able to show that they have achieved the objectives you have set for the lesson.

Most often, teachers and catechists use some sort of test or quiz to assess student learning. These tests and quizzes typically include multiple choice questions, true or false statements, fill-in-the-blanks, and sometimes short answer questions or essay questions. The problem with using *only* quizzes and tests is that their focus tends to be on performance rather than mastery. Our responsibility as religious educators is to ensure that every student continuously works toward mastery of what we teach.

Think of assessments—which include but are not limited to tests and quizzes—as indicators of student progress.

Instead of using the results of a test as the final marker of what the student has learned, use them as tools to better understand *how well* students have learned something so that you can adjust future teaching (or reteaching) to help students truly demonstrate mastery of the learning objectives. This kind of assessment is called *formative* assessment because it helps teachers craft lessons that continue to form students for the future. Remember, teaching does not stop with an assessment. An assessment is a step within the journey of learning.

Think of it this way: When you bake a cake, how do you know when it is done? You check by sticking a toothpick or a fork in it! If the cake needs more time, you put it back in the oven until it is completely cooked. Apply this lesson to teaching and assessment. Use assessments to see if students truly master the objective for the lesson. If they are "done," then you can move forward, building on what they have learned. If they need more time, then give them more opportunities to learn and demonstrate mastery of the learning objective.

## Exercise: Check Student Progress with a Formative Assessment

There are lots of examples of formative assessments. Quizzes are one form of formative assessment because they provide quick feedback of student learning, but today's challenge is to move beyond quizzes and tests. Consider using the following formative assessments in your next lesson:

- **Entrance/Exit Cards:** Ask a quick question to review the lesson and have the students write the answer on a note card as they enter the room or before they leave.

- **Thumbs Up, Thumbs Down:** As you progress through the lesson, ask students to show if they understand a topic or a question by giving you a thumbs up or a thumbs down. If you see thumbs down, spend some time individually with the students who need more help or reteach something to the entire class.

- **"I Get It" Signs:** Instead of using their thumbs, have students show how well they understand something with actual signs. These pieces of paper or cardboard could be green, yellow, and red for "I get it," "I sort of get it," and "I don't get it." Another option in the same vein are signs with three faces: one smiling, one with a flat mouth, and one frowning.

- **3-2-1:** On a blank sheet of paper (or note card), have students write *three* things they learned, *two* things they found interesting, and *one* question they still have.

- **Gist Sentences:** We've all heard the phrase, "I got the gist of it." Have students write one sentence that shows they got the gist of the day's lesson. Another variation of this would be to ask students to write a newspaper headline describing the day's lesson.

Notice how each of these formative assessment ideas can quickly reveal how well students have learned something. They give a broad idea of the percentage of students who still need help. They can be used quickly to help adjust the progress of the day's lesson. One more bonus: They do not require a lot of time to grade or correct.

## Going Deeper

Apply the parable of the Good Shepherd (Lk 15:3–7) to your relationship with your students. Recall that in the parable, ninety-nine sheep are safe and one sheep is lost. Imagine yourself as the shepherd. What thoughts or feelings are likely to go through your head as you leave ninety-nine sheep to find the one that is lost? Then think about your students. Which student is the one who needs you to leave the others to help them the most? Who else needs this extra attention? How can you spend that extra time to help this student?

# Day 23

# Simplify Your Lesson

---

*"Woe to you, scholars of the law! You have taken away the key of knowledge. You yourselves did not enter and you stopped those trying to enter." (Lk 11:52)*

Have you ever heard of the "curse of knowledge"? The curse of knowledge suggests that people who have an expertise in a certain area tend to have a difficult time explaining what they know to people who don't. There is no group of people who suffer from this more than educators.

Regardless of whether you have written a master's thesis on the topic you are teaching or you just read about it for the first time, it is likely that you already know more than your students. As religious educators, we need to strive to simplify our lessons in order to get to the core of what we teach. If we try to teach a dozen new concepts in one lesson, there is a very good chance most of the students will remember none of them shortly after leaving class. Instead, it is better to focus on core concepts. Students have a much better chance of remembering one focused lesson for the long term than a string of lessons all in one day.

There is an excellent book about how to get people to remember your message titled *Made to Stick* by Dan and Chip Heath. Their book is arranged around the acronym SUCCESs, which stands for Simple, Unexpected, Concrete, Credible, Emotional, and with Stories. Today's exercise looks at the first element: simplify the lesson. The goal will be to find the core message of a lesson and then look for ways to adapt your teaching strategies and tactics to teach that core message.

Think about how Jesus shares the Good News of salvation. He kept the message simple. "What must I do to inherit eternal life?" the rich young man asked him. Jesus told him to follow the commandments. "All of these I have observed from my youth," he replied in earnest. Jesus heard this and said, "There is still one thing left for you: sell all you have and distribute it to the poor, and you will have treasure in heaven. Then come, follow me." (Lk 18:18–22). Holiness *is* simple, but it is not easy. The challenge should be in the choice, not in the understanding.

## Exercise: Simplify Your Lesson

Apply this exercise to a lesson you will teach in the coming days. Begin by completing the following statements:

- If they learn nothing else during this lesson, they must learn . . .

- The single most important thing for students to learn in this lesson is . . .

It is not easy to set aside several important lessons for one *most* important lesson. There is just so much to teach! Most of us are given a curriculum to complete in a given semester or year, and it feels impossible to get through it all. Accept the fact that there is not enough time in the day, in the week, or in the year to teach it all. Instead, focus on getting one, clear message across to students. Would you rather your students walk away from your class with only a partial understanding of many things or a full understanding of a few very important things? Which do you think will have a bigger impact on their spiritual lives?

Imagine you are teaching a lesson about Baptism. There are many symbols associated with the sacrament. All are important and all should be introduced. But if we expect our students to really walk away with a clear understanding of the meaning of Baptism, we need to focus on one core concept. Will you focus on the water that washes away sin? Will you focus on the dying and rising we do through immersion in water? Will you focus on incorporation into the Body of Christ? Choose one concept and support it, explain it, and review it so many times the students will have to remember it.

The more you focus on one key concept in each lesson, the more you will see results in student learning. Remember that knowledge builds upon itself. When we teach, we build upon what students already know. The simpler we can make a message for students, the easier it will be to teach them more complex concepts in the weeks ahead.

## Going Deeper

The Rosary is a powerful form of prayer that contains various components. We pray a number of different prayers (Our Father, Hail Mary, the Apostles' Creed, etc.), and we meditate upon the mysteries of the lives of Christ and Mary. At its core, though, is the simple recitation of the ancient Hail Mary, calling on the Blessed Mother's intercession on our behalf. Take a few minutes today to pray and reflect on the words of the Hail Mary prayer.

# Day 24

# Tell a Story in Class

*"With many such parables he spoke the word to them as they were able to understand it." (Mk 4:33)*

Jesus had a preferred style of teaching. He told stories. His parables provide us with concrete and memorable explanations for lofty beliefs about God and his Kingdom. He filled his stories with common examples of slaves and masters, grains of wheat, mustard seeds, and banquets that easily connected with everyday experience.

Like Jesus, you can use stories to provide students with a more concrete and deeper understanding of the important topics and concepts in your lessons. The more descriptive and engaging the story, the more memorable and meaningful it will be. You do not have to be a talented storyteller for your stories to make an impact on students. Simply the presence of verbal imagery connected with real application will make a meaningful impact.

Stories can be incorporated in a variety of places within your lesson. They can be shared at the beginning of a lesson as the hook to grab students' attention. They can be used to support a claim or argument. Stories are important in another way. They can also be the basis for deepening your relationship with your students. Sharing a little piece about your life helps them to see you as a real person and make a deeper connection with you.

## Exercise: Tell a Story to Your Class

We all have stories to share. In catechesis, we are called to be witnesses to the Gospel (Day 31). This sometimes requires us to get out of our comfort zones and share stories that are personal and real, while still being appropriate.

If you're new to telling stories in class, break down the story into parts. This might seem elementary, but stories have a beginning, a middle, and an end. They describe the problem and people involved (beginning), the conflict (middle), and the resolution (end). Take the story of the prodigal son. A rich father had two sons (beginning). One son took his share of his inheritance and squandered it away (middle). The son came back to his father, who welcomed him with great joy while the other son jealously complained (end). When you choose a story you will tell for today's exercise, likewise break it down into three parts to help get your message across.

As part of the Day 20 exercise, you considered why a particular lesson was important to you. In a similar way, think of a story for your next lesson that shows how the topic or the lesson of the day can be given a deeper meaning. Look to the following sources for stories to tell:

**Personal life.** Connect a personal story or memory that relates to the lesson and might help frame the importance of what you are teaching. Use a story that is more than just an anecdotal memory. Make sure to include how this particular experience changed your life even in just a little way. For example, if you are teaching a lesson about the Eucharist, share a memorable experience you had at Mass in the recent or distant past.

**Current events.** There are so many things going on in the world today that connect with matters of faith. What are the current events that everyone is talking about and that your students are certainly aware of? Retell the story to get all of the students on the same page. Then make connections between the events and the lesson of the day.

**Films.** What age-appropriate films can help support the lesson of the day? You could certainly show a clip of a film to illustrate the point, but make sure you also do make a connection between the film clip and the lesson with a story that sets up the scene or makes a good follow-up point. It is the explanation of the story and the connection that you make to the lesson as a teacher that will have the biggest impact on learning.

**Fairy tales.** Children's fairy tales in and of themselves have important lessons. Retelling them for school-age students can help them appreciate those lessons in a new way. Retell a fairy tale or have the students help you read or act out the story as a class. Make connections between the fairy tale and the lesson of the day, or ask the students to make connections themselves.

**Scripture.** The Bible is different from any other book. As God's Word, it is a living document. Reading and hearing stories from the Bible impact us in new and different ways each time. For this exercise, if you choose to share a story from the Bible, be sure to actually *tell* a story. Don't assume students know the story even if you have already read it together as a class. Provide some context to the story and retell it in its entirety to help students see the connections between it and the lesson of the day.

## Going Deeper

Put yourself within a story in the Bible. For example, imagine that you are the prodigal son in Luke 15:11–32. What thoughts and feelings might you have as a person in that story? How would you act differently? What memories and lessons would you have to share with others if you were to recount the story in a first-person retelling?

# Day 25

# Change the Way Your Students Read Their Textbook

*"You shall indeed hear but not understand . . . but blessed are your eyes, because they see, and your ears, because they hear." (Mt 13:14, 16)*

Textbooks are essential tools in religious education. Most dioceses, schools, and parishes require the use of textbooks that are in conformity with the *Catechism of the Catholic Church*, as determined by a committee of the United States Conference of Catholic Bishops.

Textbooks are one tool that should be used as part of a greater catechetical program within your classroom. Having an approved textbook is important, but it does not automatically make it easy to use as a teaching tool. Textbook publishers do their best to create textbooks at the appropriate grade level, but teachers must adapt them "to the capacity of the learners" and present them in a way "that can be understood" by students (*NDC*, 283). Teacher and catechist manuals provide helpful ideas for teaching the content.

As religious educators, our work and our witness (Day 31) play the central role in catechesis. This includes helping our students manage the textbook. Students still need to be motivated to read the book and understand the material. It is our job as the teachers and catechists to make this happen. When a student does not read the book, we have a tendency to blame them for laziness and neglect. If they read and fail to retain what they have read, we again direct the blame toward the students. This is wrong. It is our job to motivate the students to read and help them retain what they have read. Remember, you are a servant, not a task-master.

## Exercise: Help Students Effectively Read and Retain Information from the Textbook

Think for a moment about the common components of a textbook. Your class textbook is likely to have chapters, headings, subheads, pictures, graphs, vocabulary definitions, and review questions. Sometimes textbooks will have student objectives, project ideas, reflection prompts, and summary points. These are all essential elements to help students effectively read and understand the main text. As teachers we need to use these components of the textbook to our advantage by drawing attention to them and helping students use them to make connections and summarize the main text that they are assigned to read.

Reading is more than just an event; it is a process that includes preparation, engagement, and reflection. Before reading, students should prepare by making predictions and asking questions about what they will read. With that context in mind, reading becomes an active search for answers rather than a passive reception of ideas. Afterward, students should reflect on what they have read by challenging themselves to remember ideas and information while still fresh in their memories. They should also begin to think critically about what they have learned.

There are a number of reading strategies and graphic organizers to help facilitate a reading process. Consider using the following ideas with your students:

- **Pre-reading habits.** Teach students to habitually spend time reviewing what they will read before they read it. Textbooks are not novels. There is no way to ruin the ending! Before students read new material, ask them to survey the chapter title, headings and subheads, pictures, vocabulary words, and the first and last sentence of each paragraph or section. Then have them make predictions or ask questions about what they will read.

- **SQ3R.** This method of reading is often used in conjunction with a graphic organizer that has students Survey (S); Question (Q); and Read, Recite, and Review (3R) the textbook. Before reading, students *survey* the material and ask *questions* about what they think they will read. While they *read*, students take notes and answer the questions they posed. After reading the textbook, they *recite* the questions and answers they formed and *review* their notes.

- **Taking notes.** Many students like to highlight and take notes. But are they doing so in the most effective way? Taking notes has to be taught like any other learning skill. One way to facilitate effective note-taking is to provide some guided notes or questions for students to complete while they read. You can also model effective highlighting and underlining by sampling how they should choose the most important information or summary sentences in each paragraph or section.

- **Review.** How many of us have started a new class asking students questions about what they have read the night before only to be met with blank stares? It is okay to give students the chance to review what they have read by giving in-class assignments and questions to help fuel a discussion about the book. Remember, our goal is not to test and reward students who perform well. We should test and reteach the students who need more help (see Day 22).

## Going Deeper

Apply some of the methods in this exercise to your own personal study of the Bible. Take a chapter, section, or even a whole book or letter in the Bible and spend some time pre-reading, reading for comprehension, and reviewing what you have read.

# Day 26

# **Plan and Assign a Project**

*"He spoke to them another parable. 'The kingdom of heaven is like yeast that a woman took and mixed with three measures of wheat flour until the whole batch was leavened.'" (Mt 13:33)*

Today you will be asked to think for the long-term. Assigning projects for students to apply what they have learned takes time and energy for both the student and the educator. Projects take days and possibly weeks for a student to complete. They should also take a significant amount of time on the part of the teacher to assess and measure student learning based on the completed project. Because of the time involved for both students and teachers, projects should not be assigned without an awareness of that fact.

The advancements of technology have conditioned both students and teachers to expect instant answers and short-term results for work that we do. To spend multiple hours working on a project is not an easy thing to do, especially for young people.

For our purposes, a project is defined as "an assignment that challenges students to think critically about what they have learned." Research projects are great, but unless you will also teach how to do proper research and will assess them on those researching skills, the assignments will not automatically reinforce your learning objectives. Instead, remember projects that focus on mastering an objective and measuring progress toward that mastery (see Days 21 and 22). Think of projects as refining that mastery in real and authentic ways.

There is another benefit of assigning long-term projects. While some students are working on their projects in class, you can spend time with other students who are still working toward the mastery of certain objectives. You will have the chance to spend the necessary amount of time reteaching these students and getting them prepared to do well on the project and the rest of the course work as well.

## Exercise: Plan and Assign a Project

Take some time to plan a long-term project using the steps listed in this exercise. You may not actually assign it today, but you can start to prepare students for the assignment by reviewing some of the important content that they need to know to complete the project.

**First, examine a set of learning objectives from the past few weeks or in the weeks ahead.** How can these lessons be strung together for one big goal? Often textbooks will be organized into units. Consider using that structure to help you decide what larger goal, connected with a set of lessons, can serve as the basis for a project. Ideally, you will begin to set this larger goal when planning ahead for a set of lessons.

**Write out a unit goal.** Use the same structure presented in Day 21, but make sure that this goal requires critical thinking. Use verbs or verb phrases like *compare and contrast, evaluate, make connections, design, plan, make a prediction, create a criteria for, form a conclusion, predict, prioritize, select the best way to, rate,* etc. This unit goal will require mastery of multiple learning objectives. In other words, it would be difficult for students to compare two concepts if they didn't know enough about the concepts individually first. Similarly, it would be impossible for you to evaluate something the students didn't understand.

**Brainstorm a list of projects to match up with the unit goal.** Some project ideas are:

- Developing and acting out a role play (*make connections*)

- Writing a first-person narrative in the words of one of the people the students learned about in class (*select the best way to*)

- Writing an extension of a story or part of the text as if they were the author (*make predictions*)

The best kinds of projects creatively and authentically connect with what students have already learned.

**Choose one project and write out the step-by-step process to complete it.** What knowledge is necessary to complete each step of the project? What materials will students need to complete the project? What will you need to create for them? What are the steps necessary to complete this project? How much time will each step take? What will you need to review with them in order for students to master the skills?

**Design a rubric to measure student work.** A rubric is a tool that you can use to measure students' work as excellent (4), good (3), satisfactory (2), unsatisfactory (1), or incomplete (0). Break down the project into different parts and describe examples (excellent, good, satisfactory, and unsatisfactory examples) of each part to measure. In a class debate, for example, you might measure the individual work students completed in preparation for the debate as well as participation in the debate itself. *Excellent participation* would involve both listening and speaking, *good participation* might be speaking and listening but somewhat off-topic or less focused, *satisfactory participation* might be just showing good listening skills, and *unsatisfactory participation* would be exhibited by students who are inattentive and disengaged from the discussion.

Rubrics are very important even if you do not use them for individual letter grades. They help students understand your expectations as a teacher. This way they do not spend hours designing a project that will not illustrate the intended learning.

As an alternative to assigning individual projects that demonstrate mastery of learning objectives, consider planning an all-class service project that is related to what they are learning. You could certainly measure what they have learned as part of the project, but do your best to use the service itself as motivation rather than grades or the pursuit of community service hours.

## Going Deeper

We tend to avoid projects that take multiple days to complete because we would rather enjoy the short-term

pleasures of TV, social media, e-mail, and other easily completed tasks. Do you have a long-term project that you are
working on? It may be a part of your work as a religious
educator, or it could be a project that is taking days to
complete around the house or at another job. Spend some
time working on that project today.

# Day 27

# Incorporate Music into Your Day

*"It is good to give thanks to the LORD,*
*to sing praise to your name, Most High,*
*To proclaim your love in the morning,*
*your faithfulness in the night,*
*With the ten-stringed harp,*
*with melody upon the lyre." (Ps 92:2–4)*

Remember, the aim of catechesis is to put our students not only in touch with but in communion and intimacy with Jesus Christ. Music has a particular power to touch our hearts and awaken within us emotions and memories that are too powerful to ignore.

My wife recently got an e-mail from a former fourth-grade student of hers who is now in high school. What did the student remember most about her experience in fourth grade? The music. This former student was so thankful for the praise and worship songs they sang in class. It left a lasting impression on her and a fond memory of the class experience.

Music has a pedagogical value that is so subtle we often miss it. I'll never forget the first day my then-two-year-old daughter sang the *Gloria* while she was playing with her toys. When young people sing songs of faith, they retain a deeper understanding than can ever be communicated through written or spoken word.

Do you ever consider how music impacts your own day? Music offers a crucial background to television, movies, our time alone in the car, or jogging along with our earphones. The emotional effect music has on us is important not to forget. Why not embrace music as religious educators?

How have you used music as a part of class prayer? Do you consider the positive effect it has on your students as individuals and as a group? There truly are a number of benefits to using music in class. The *National Directory for Catechesis* describes music in this way: "Sacred music invites the faithful to give glory to God: it enhances their prayer, fosters the unity of their minds and hearts, and aims to draw them closer to Christ" (*NDC*, 151).

# Exercise: Incorporate Music into Your Lesson Today

There are several ways to incorporate music into a classroom experience. For today's exercise, choose and try one or more of the following uses of music: memorization, praise and worship, meditation, or inspiration.

**Memorization.** A chant is a well-known technique used to memorize important facts, rules, and formulas in math. This can be a very effective use of music in religious education as well. Songs can also be used to help students remember prayers. Music and well-known tunes like "Twinkle, Twinkle Little Star," "The Itsy-Bitsy Spider," and "Happy Birthday to You" can all be great tools to help memorize facts and lists. This can come in handy if you are asking students to memorize things like the seven sacraments, the names of the books in the Bible, the gifts of the Holy Spirit, or the names of the twelve Apostles. Try making up a song using a well-known tune to memorize a list of facts about your lesson today.

**Praise and worship.** There are a number of benefits to praise-and-worship music, that is, lively music with catchy lyrics and a good rhythm all intended to express joy in knowing and loving God. First, students of all ages tend to enjoy this kind of music. Second, it appeals to multiple types of intelligences when the music is matched with hand motions and dances. Third, it gets students out of their comfort zones. As a result, students tend to see the classroom as a place where they can feel comfortable with themselves. Realizing that no one laughed at them when they sang or did the hand motions of a praise-and-worship song will help students to feel more comfortable participating in other ways in class.

**Reflection and meditation.** Playing quiet, spiritual music is a perfect way to help set the mood for reflective prayer. Just as music can set the emotional tone in the background of a movie, it can also set the emotional tone in the background of prayer.

**Inspiration.** If you've been on a retreat, either as a leader or when you were a teen, recall how music played an important part. At the end of witness talks, student leaders typically pick music to further connect their talks with the lives of the retreatants. These songs serve as inspiration that touch the heart and encourage conversation. In the same way, consider selecting a song that can have an emotional effect on your students. Have them listen to and reflect on the song itself as a source of inspiration for their day.

Take a look at the next lesson you will teach. Set aside some time for music in your lesson plan. Look for the kinds of music you want to play on the Internet, on YouTube, or as a download. Ask your school or parish if they have CDs with the types of songs you are hoping to play. Then, incorporate music into your lesson plan.

## Going Deeper

In your own personal prayer today, choose a song for personal reflection. Next, clear your head of thoughts and worries. Play the song and let it guide your thoughts and feelings. Take a few moments after the song is over to reflect on your own life and its connection to that particular song.

# Day 28

# Liberate Students from Their Chairs

---

*"Suddenly an angel of the Lord stood by him and a light shone in the cell. He tapped Peter on the side and awakened him, saying, 'Get up quickly.' The chains fell from his wrists." (Acts 12:7)*

We are in a constant battle to keep our students' attention. If they are getting restless, it is a good sign that they need to move around. Most young people need this movement so much more than they are allowed to have. The more we build in constructive opportunities for movement, the more attentive and engaged they can be.

Think about the way preschoolers learn. Preschool teachers use a lot of music coupled with dance and hand motions to teach lessons. Most of us still remember the hand motions and dances we learned as children. You likely remember the hand motions for this popular rhyme: "Here is the church. Here is the steeple. Open it up and here are the people."

Hand motions and movement help us make memories. Why should the way older students learn be that much different?

Plan for some movement in today's lesson. Do not feel like you need to abandon chairs and organized rows or sets of desks for the entire class period. Just be sure to mix it up and provide activities with movement. Young people do need to move their bodies!

We often underestimate the potential in bodily-kinesthetic learning. Kinesthetic learning appeals to the part of our intelligence that needs movement. Kinesthetic learning allows students to carry out some physical activity with their hands or their feet rather than listening, writing, talking, or watching. It is one of the learning styles described in Howard Gardner's theory of multiple intelligences.

Getting students out of their chairs is a good start, but getting them out of the classroom can also be productive from time to time. Interrupting the common, repeatable surroundings will help open up students' minds to some new creative thinking. That is why some of the suggestions in the exercise today extend beyond the classroom.

## Exercise: Liberate Students from Their Chairs

When introducing any of the following suggestions for adding movement to your lesson, be sure to maintain normal classroom procedures (Day 15) and rules (Day 16). Remind students of these procedures and rules before introducing any of the following activities:

**Learning centers.** Set up various learning centers (or stations) around the room. Make the focus of each station an activity that students can work on alone or in groups. Your role is to move from station to station, group to group, to help students who are struggling the most. Fellow classmates can also help each other. After a designated amount of time, have students rotate to a different station with a new activity.

**Games.** Students love playing games in class. Introduce some games that require students to use their bodies and get out of their chairs.

**Take a stance.** Post signs in the four corners of the room labeled *Strongly Agree*, *Agree*, *Disagree*, and *Strongly Disagree*. Read debatable statements related to the day's lesson and have students move to one of the four corners that represents their stance on the issue. Pause with each question and discuss why they have the opinions they do.

**Praise-and-worship motions.** After Day 27, you may already be including praise-and-worship music in your lesson. Now make sure to get the students out of their chairs and use the hand motions to go along with these songs.

**Take a field trip to the church or chapel.** Spend part of your class in the school or parish chapel or church. Use this time for personal or communal prayer, or help students meditate upon a certain Catholic symbol displayed in a stained glass window, painting, or statue.

**Go outside.** If the weather is nice, take students outside for some prayerful reflection. Make this time productive, though, or do not do it at all. Do not let students interpret this as an opportunity to be free from learning completely. Give specific instructions for what you would like them to accomplish while they are outside. Do this at your own risk, for students will ask to go outside on every nice day for the rest of the year if you are not careful!

## Going Deeper

Do some physical exercise today. What does this have to do with becoming a better religious educator? Exercise helps us think more clearly. Exercise can open up ourselves to creativity that we may not otherwise reach. Go on a ten-minute walk around the block. Go for a run. Do some push-ups or jumping jacks. Get your body moving and see how this impacts you as a teacher and as a person.

# Day 29

# **Review a Lesson from the Past**

*"And Mary kept all these things, reflecting on them in her heart." (Lk 2:19)*

Let's face it: Our lives are incredibly busy. There is always more to do and never enough time. When we finish one task, it is time to move on to the next. We act like we don't want to think about the lesson we just completed ever again. Rarely do we take the time to review our lessons and the impact they had on our students.

Do not underestimate the value of reviewing your performance as a teacher. Learn a lesson from football coaches who pour hours of time into reviewing game film to find the areas where they can make their teams better. They find the bright spots, the plays that show perfect execution of some skill or strategy. They also look for the missteps, the poor technique, and the mental errors that led to losses. The purpose of this time is to think about how the mistakes and the successes can be used to improve performance in the future.

Just as it can be hard to relive a lesson you taught that went poorly, so, too, is it hard for coaches to review game film from a losing game. But they know that recognizing the reasons for success or failure is the only way to get better in the future. On Day 22 we focused on assessment as a tool to measure student progress so we can continue to reteach or extend what students have learned so far. In a similar way, today you will focus on your performance as a teacher and commit to making improvements that will make you a better religious educator in the days ahead.

Assuming you will teach some variation of your most recent lesson again in a future term, likely a year or more away, the act of reflection and review will have a big impact on how well you teach it the next time. In your lesson planning template or planning book, designate a spot for writing notes for reflection that you can reference in the future. Give yourself some advice on how to teach this lesson again so you are not guessing about how well things went the first time you taught it.

# Exercise: Review a Previous Lesson Plan

Take ten minutes to reflect deeply on a lesson you recently taught. Answer these three questions:

- What went well?

- What didn't go well?

- What would I change if I had to do it again?

Take a piece of paper and divide it into two halves labeled "The Bright Spots" (or, "What went well?") and "The Room for Improvement" (or, "What didn't go well?"). Then at the bottom save some room for "Changes" (or, "What would I change if I had to do it again?") that you would make for your next lesson or the next time you teach this particular topic. Write down your answers to these questions for each section. Here are some of the areas that you should focus on during your review:

**Start with student engagement.** Look for bright spots. When were the students engaged in either what you said or what they were doing? Note room for improvement by answering the following: When were students getting off-task, day-dreaming, talking out, or confused? Plan to make some changes. What activities would you eliminate next time and what might you add instead?

**Focus on your delivery.** Were your instructions clear (see Day 14)? If you lectured, were your thoughts concise and organized (see Day 23)? Did you check in often enough with students to make sure they were making progress toward the learning objective (see Day 14)? Could you have incorporated story (Day 24), music (Day 27), or movement (Day 27) in some additional way to help students learn?

**Consider outside factors.** Success or failure is not always in our control. What were some of the outside factors that contributed to the way a lesson went? Was it a Friday afternoon? Was it getting close to Christmas or summer break? Were you feeling tired or ill? Were some of your students having a particularly bad day? Make a note of this on your two-columned paper or lesson plan.

Use the days in this book as a guide. Review the exercises in this book, particularly those in parts III and IV. Take a look at your learning objectives, your assessments, your stories, the music you played, the reading strategies you used, etc. Which of these needs to be revamped and updated? Consider going back and doing one of the exercises from this book again in the future.

You can download a template for this exercise at www.thereligionteacher.com/31days/day29.

## Going Deeper

A popular prayer from St. Ignatius of Loyola can help you to review your day. In his *Spiritual Exercises*, St. Ignatius of Loyola suggested that the Prayer of Examen be practiced twice daily in order to reflect and give thanks. St. Ignatius suggested a process in which we do the following:

1. Give thanks
2. Ask for the Holy Spirit's guidance
3. Review the day
4. Ask for grace and forgiveness
5. Repent

Apply these five steps to help you review your day.

# Day 30

# Visualize a Lesson in Action

---

*"Entrust your works to the Lord,*
*and your plans will succeed." (Prv 16:3)*

There was a recent study that measured the success rate of basketball players who *visualized* shooting free throws versus those who actually *shot* free throws without visualization. Dr. Blaslotto of the University of Chicago found that the group that visualized making free throws improved just as much as those who practiced shooting free throws every day for an hour!

To visualize something in the future is to focus on your senses and feelings as you perform some task. So in the basketball study, players would be imagining their surroundings, the rim, and the feel of the ball in their hands. They could imagine the smell of the leather from the ball as they lifted it up to shoot. They would take into account the sounds of other players positioning themselves for a rebound or fans making noise to distract them. They would then focus on the mechanics of how they shot the ball and ask themselves: Where do I aim? What do my feet and legs do? How are my hands positioned? What kind of release will I carry out?

This same habit of visualization can be applied to teaching. We spend so much time planning and preparing for our lessons, but we usually execute them without practice. We need to visualize our lessons before we give them, running through in our minds as many things that can go right and some of the things that might go wrong as well. In Day 29 we looked back on a previous lesson to improve our teaching. Today we will look at a future lesson to prepare for any obstacles in order to deliver the best possible lesson for our students.

## Exercise: Visualize a Lesson in Action

President Abraham Lincoln is credited with saying, "Give me six hours to chop down a tree and I will spend the first four sharpening the axe." In today's exercise you will spend this time sharpening your axe by visualizing how you will execute a future lesson. Consider the following methods of visualization:

**Review your next lesson plan.** Start by reviewing the lesson plan you have prepared for the next class session. Visualize yourself during each activity. Imagine the words you will speak to introduce each part of the lesson. Focus on the details. Where will you stand? Who will you see? Visualize the students in their assigned or typical seats listening to you and your words. Visualize the students participating in each portion of the lesson. Make note of the parts of the lesson where you and they are likely to have challenges. Understand how the lesson will go, but also how you and your students will react to obstacles (e.g., getting off task, finishing early, etc.).

**Focus on the challenges.** Now that you have reviewed the entire lesson plan in your mind, go back to the spots that will be most challenging for the students. Visualize all the possible reactions to the activity you have planned. What questions can you prepare for them to ask? Who will be asking them? Imagine yourself correcting the students, helping the students, and answering their questions. Be specific in your visualization. Which students do you expect to ask for help? Which students will need help but not ask for it? How will you step in to make sure everyone does well?

**Visualize yourself in the students' shoes.** This step goes even deeper. Imagine that you are one of your students. How would you feel during the different parts of the lesson? What would you really be thinking and feeling? What parts of the lesson would you be engaged in the most? Which part of the lesson would you wish you did not have to do? Then, shifting back to visualizing yourself as the teacher, how can you prepare for and address those thoughts and feelings?

**Make changes to the lesson plan if necessary.** Now that you have spent the time visualizing your lesson, you may need to go back and add resources or steps for instructions. Or, you may want to adjust the assignments you have prepared or makes notes about how you want to deliver it. Take a few minutes to do this before actually teaching the lesson.

This exercise can also be applied to other parts of your day as a religious educator. If you are experiencing some difficulties in transition from one class period to the next, or having problems escorting students from your room to another location (lunch, recess, Mass, the library, the auditorium, etc.), then try visualizing the challenges before they come up. Visualize yourself correcting student misbehavior when it occurs. Consider how you will prepare students for the noninstructional moments of your day.

## Going Deeper

Apply this method of visualization to prayer or liturgy. Before sitting to pray the Rosary or some other devotional practice, visualize yourself in prayer. What will you meditate on? What will you be feeling? In preparation for Mass, imagine your disposition and thoughts during the readings, during the eucharistic prayer, and while receiving Communion. Do the same in preparation for the Sacrament of Reconciliation as part of an examination of conscience.

# Day 31

# Become a Witness

*"But you will receive power when the holy Spirit comes upon you, and you will be my witnesses in Jerusalem, throughout Judea and Samaria, and to the ends of the earth." (Acts 1:8)*

Of all the days and exercises, this final day is the most important. Most of this book has been focused on teaching strategies and tactics that will help you perform better in the classroom, but there are no strategies or lesson plans or activities that will compare to the impact we have on our students as living witnesses to the Gospel of Jesus Christ. *You* are the best teaching strategy. Nothing you do in class can compare to your faithful commitment to Christ as a living witness to the Gospel. Pope Paul VI wrote that people are "more willing to listen to witnesses than to teachers" and added that if someone does listen to a teacher, it is because the teacher is also a witness (*Evangelii Nuntiandi*, 41).

No matter who we are, as baptized Christians we, too, are called to be witnesses each and every day. The Latin word for witness is *martyr*. Modeled on the early Christian martyrs who put God before their own lives, teachers are also witnesses who take up their own crosses and follow Jesus. We are called to experience little deaths to our wants and needs. We also do this when we take joy in God's will rather than our own intentions and desires.

In a special way, the call to witness is at the center of the call to teach. "The effectiveness of religious instruction is closely tied to the personal witness given by the teacher; this witness is what brings the content of the lessons to life" (*NDC*, 232). Let us not limit catechesis to methods, resources, books, or even the *Catechism of the Catholic Church*! Catechesis must focus on the mystery of Christ. We experience this mystery as an encounter with the living God, both in his Word and in his people. Having encountered this mystery ourselves, we are called to bear witness to it. Your witness to the person of Christ, who actively changes your life each day, is more important than anything else you do as a religious educator.

This means that every day you must live a life walking side by side with Jesus in prayer, thought, word, and deed. It means humbling yourself as a servant and disciple so that you can truly be an effective teacher and leader. It means seeking to learn from Christ. It means serving his people. To do all this requires ongoing conversion. To be true witnesses each day you must take on a habit of openness to God's grace so that you constantly turn back to him. In turn, you can help your students grow into disciples of Christ and witnesses to the Good News.

## Exercise: Become a Witness

Like so many of the exercises in this book, this final day of this thirty-one-day journey is something we should practice each and every day. We are called to be witnesses not out of an obligation or command, but as a result of our constant conversion toward Christ.

To become a witness, we go through a conversion PROCESS that is represented by the acronym itself:

**P**: Prior Experience

**R**: Receive Grace

**O**: Openness to Grace

**C**: Conversion

**ESS**: Witness

This is the process you have experienced in order to become the witness you are today. It is also the process we take our students through in any form of religious education. We begin with the life experiences we have had leading up to this moment. Then, we receive grace by an encounter with God in various ways, whether it is in Scripture, in other people, in prayer, in the sacraments, in our thoughts, in our actions, in our gifts, or in the works of the Church. We receive this grace no matter how open we are to it, but the measure by which this grace has an effect on us is related to the openness we have to it. This openness leads us into the moment of conversion. Our openness invites God to change our hearts. This change leads unavoidably to our becoming a living witness. We witness to the Christ who has changed us.

For today's exercise, think of one of your most powerful religious experiences—what some might call a conversion experience. Consider how each part of the conversion PROCESS applies to that experience:

- What **prior experiences** did you bring to this event, whether they are emotional baggage, challenging events, ways of living, etc.?

- By what encounter with God did you **receive grace**? Was it in the sacraments, prayer, Scripture, another person, a retreat, or some other way?

- In what ways were you **open to the grace** of the encounter? Were you praying? Were you surrounded by other supportive believers? Did you give up on your own efforts to change your situation?

- How would you describe the moment of **conversion**? What changed within you? What is it that you could not keep to yourself?

- How have you been a **witness** of this conversion for others? How did your life change? How did you see the world differently? How did you act differently? How have you shared this with others?

This is the conversion PROCESS experience you are to share with your students. The more you accept this plan to continually change your life, the more you can change the lives of others. This is the path of the disciple-teacher. This is why you can always become a better religious educator, no matter how good you are now.

Your students need your inspiration. They need you to live the life you were meant to live. They need to be transformed by Christ just as you were transformed by Christ. Take up this call to teach through discipleship. Become the leader you were meant to be through unselfish service to the children in your care.

May God bless you and your ministry. May he inspire you to be a living witness today, tomorrow, and each day for the rest of your life.

## Going Deeper

Who are the witnesses in your life? How did they communicate their own experience and love for God to you? What experiences changed lives? What virtues do they exemplify? How can you be more like them?

Founded in 1865, Ave Maria Press,
a ministry of the Congregation of
Holy Cross, is a Catholic publishing
company that serves the spiritual and
formative needs of the Church and its
schools, institutions, and ministers;
Christian individuals and families; and
others seeking spiritual nourishment.

———————

For a complete listing of titles from

Ave Maria Press

Sorin Books

Forest of Peace

Christian Classics

visit www.avemariapress.com

**ave maria press®** / Notre Dame, IN 46556
A Ministry of the United States Province of Holy Cross

**Jared Dees** is digital publishing specialist at Ave Maria Press. He is creator of the popular website *The Religion Teacher*, which provides practical resources and effective teaching strategies to religious educators. A respected graduate of the Alliance for Catholic Education (ACE) program at the University of Notre Dame, Dees holds master's degrees in education and theology, both from Notre Dame. He has taught in Catholic schools and parish religious education programs, and his articles have appeared in *Momentum*, *Today's Parish*, and on numerous websites. Dees lives in South Bend, Indiana, with his wife and three children.